a year

and

six

seconds

also by Isabel Gillies

Happens Every Day

a year
and
six
seconds

a love story

Isabel Gillies

voice

Hyperion | New York

A note to readers:

This book is a work of nonfiction. Some of the names and details, however, have been changed. It is the memory of a time in my life that happened years ago, but I have recounted it to the best of my ability and with the full understanding that there are always two sides to every story.

Good Lovin'
Words and Music by Rudy Clark and Arthur Resnick
Copyright © 1965 by Alley Music Corp. and Bug Music-Trio Music Company
Copyright Renewed
International Copyright Secured All Rights Reserved
Used by Permission of Alley Music Corporation
Reprinted by permission of Hal Leonard Corporation

Library of Congress Cataloging-in-Publication Data

Gillies, Isabel
    A year and six seconds : a love story / Isabel Gillies.—1st ed.
        p. cm.
    ISBN 978-1-4013-4162-6
    1. Gillies, Isabel, 1970–   2. Actors—United States—Biography.
    I. Title.
    PN2287.G5175A3 2011
    792.02'8092—dc22
    [B]

                                                    2010053486

Hyperion books are available for special promotions and premiums. For details contact the HarperCollins Special Markets Department in the New York office at 212-207-7528, fax 212-207-7222, or email spsales@harpercollins.com.

Book design by Fearn Cutler de Vicq

FIRST EDITION

10 9 8 7 6 5 4 3 2 1

THIS LABEL APPLIES TO TEXT STOCK

For Peter, and our beloved children

"Well turn on your light, you won't regret it,
You've got to go for the good and get it."
—"GOOD LOVIN'" AS SUNG BY THE GRATEFUL DEAD

"In the cosmos, there is no refuge from change."
—CARL SAGAN

a year

and

six

seconds

prologue

D id you know that it only takes six seconds to fall in love?
A friend told me there's a new study out that proves
it. Thank goodness science has weighed in on love at first
sight, because I have always loved that human faculty. I believe in it. Six-second love has happened to me. More than
once. I'm not talking about a fleeting thought about how
someone is hot, and I'm not talking about a crush; I'm talking
about knowing with certainty that you could spend your life
with this person. In an instant, not only are you down the
aisle, but you have had the babies, you have reached old age,
and you are buried side by side under a tree for all eternity. In
six seconds, you see it all. And you feel it; you feel the love that
will make your whole life shift. Six-second love is real, but it
doesn't always get you to happily ever after. With one of my
loves, I got to the married part and through the babies part,
then we divorced.

And right after you hear the words "I don't want to be
married to you anymore," there is another kind of time, a

transition time. Everyone will handle this period differently, and it will vary in length from one person to the next, but it has a beginning, middle, and end. I'm not saying that you will ever be over the breakup of your marriage. Any relationship that started with that six-second love stays with you forever, and that is as it should be. Like everything else in this life, it changes constantly—it subsides, flares, grows distant, comes close, gets smooth—but, make no mistake, it stays. Meanwhile, the reconstruction of your life happens within a distinct time, during which you pick up your chin, dust off your jeans, collect your belongings, look around at where you have landed. If you have children, you hold them close until they get their bearings. It is a natural time to make lists and organize yourself into being okay. It is also a time to look inside and find out if there is the possibility for even *more change*. This transformation can be painful, as it often begins when you are wrecked and tender, but it can be extraordinary, too. Even by taking the smallest steps forward, you grow and learn—and to quote the genius Carl Sagan, "Understanding is joyous." This is an important time, and for me, that time was a year.

Somewhere in the middle of that year, I fell in love again, in six seconds. That's what happened. And a while after that, I found myself on a road to happiness.

part

I

chapter 1

I thought for sure the boys would make him stay. They are the best things I ever had a hand in creating (if one can even take credit for that kind of thing), and if the two of them plus my most sincere and thought-through arguments for our life together didn't convince him that leaving me was a bad idea, I couldn't think of anything else that would. Truthfully, he probably would have taken the boys, but I couldn't bear that, and we both agreed it didn't make sense for me to stay where we lived, so, stunned and sad, I left behind our long-dreamed-for, recently renovated house, and our beloved, small college town in Oberlin, Ohio, taking our little ones home to the apartment where I grew up, to live with my parents in New York City.

I'd never imagined ending up in the nutty situation I found myself in, carting toddlers, Wallace and James, with only one precious book and one lovey apiece, on an airplane, by myself and separated, to New York, in the middle of what should have been the jolly Christmas season, *to live with my parents,* wedding ringless (and in the place of the ring was an inexplicable, angry rash), exhausted and humiliated from countless conversations about *what happened* (unclear) and "*the other woman*" (also unclear), shaken from banging out custody plans with someone I still loved, and humbled by talking with my poor mother about where the diapers would go in the boys' new room in Apartment 7A. The only thing I could think (except for images of Meryl Streep at the end of *Heartburn* or even Berger marching onto the plane in the final moments of *Hair*) while standing in the taxi line at dreary LaGuardia Airport, one arm wrapped around a baby who desperately needed to be changed and the other holding the hand of an almost-four-year-old in an unbearably sweet but ill-fitting (because it was a hand-me-down, from my sister-in-law) loden coat, was: *Crikey.*

chapter 2

"Crikey" is my mother's word. I think it was my grandfather's word, too, but my mother always uses it in times
of *wow-this-is-a-pickle-and-I-don't-know-what-to-do-about-it.* Anything from leaving the oven on to something much more serious, like a divorce, gets a "crikey."

I was going home to the apartment where I grew up to find
out what on earth the rest of our life was going to be besides a
wild and deeply sad reality. My marriage, which I had treasured, was gone.

"Oh, HELLO! . . . hello . . . ," my mother called, then she
softened as she got closer to me, her arms went up and then
fell around my shoulders, kissing me on both sides of my face.
She had a kitchen timer in one hand, as if she had just been
setting it. "Goodness . . . what a trip . . . Come in, my darlings."

"Hi, guyz-ies!" my dad bent down and cheerfully said to his
grandsons. "How was *the plane?*" He wrapped one arm around
me and squeezed.

The apartment was done up for the holidays, tall boughs of

white pine on the piano, the crèche set up with kings, lambs, and the Holy Family, but everywhere there was also evidence that my parents had been rearranging their lives to prepare for an unknowable, intimidating chapter. A wrench had been tossed into my life, but I saw right then, across my mother's shoulders as she hugged me and I looked out from the front hall and into the living room, that my parents were getting a wrench as big as a city bus tossed into their lives, too. At the far end of the room, where there had once been a window bench and two French bergère upholstered chairs, with plenty of space for sitting quietly, there now were neatly piled puzzles, a low preschool-like table for Legos and blocks—and alongside the table *were* the Legos and the blocks; also, a bin of 1970s Matchbox cars that had once belonged to my brother Andrew, and an ugly, plastic carpenter tools set in primary colors. The far end of my parents' living room looked like the set of *Romper Room*.

My mother is the kind of person who anticipates the basic needs of travelers, especially of travelers who are in some kind of trauma. The first need very well might be for a hot bath, and not any old bath. In the corner where the rounded, old tub meets the bathroom wall, there will be a little glass bottle of Floris Florissa bath oil, like a potion from the Good Witch. You need only shake the tiniest drop under the tap to fill the room with a heady, woodsy, transforming fragrance. I always used to think queens would use that stuff. Any remnant sense of troubling airport travel or a too-cold day or a bad dream evaporates when that brew mixes in with the hot water around you.

A long soak will usually be followed by a good meal. This

kind of thinking is instinctive for my mother. I bet you the moment she knew the date we would be arriving she had self-soothed by planning the menus for a first-night-home dinner—one menu for the grown-ups and one for the small children. In my family, the children, because of bedtimes, almost always eat first and in the kitchen. This might sound rigid and formal, and maybe it did come out of a children-must-be-seen-and-not-heard time in the past, but it is actually cozy. At least one adult is always there to sit and talk with the children, pour more milk, maybe give a gentle reminder of manners, and also stir or chop something the older generation will be having for dinner later. When I was little, suppertime in our small Upper West Side kitchen was warm and smelled of browning onions and Uncle Ben's rice.

Sure enough, soon after we arrived from Ohio, I saw in the kitchen that a little blue-painted table with little blue-painted chairs—an eerie duplicate of the table my brother and I had shared when we were small—had been set with dessert forks on folded paper napkins and with small juice glasses for milk. The boys' meal of chicken cutlets, peas, and rice waited on the stove, ready to be served as soon as my parents and I ushered them in to sit down.

On a shelf directly above the little table was, as there had always been, a line of identical, clear glass jars, like jars you might see in an old-fashioned mercantile. The lids of the jars looked like chunky hats, with perfectly proportioned, smooth glass pompoms on top so you could open and close each one easily. Inside the jars were flour, brown sugar, white sugar, beans, cornmeal, dried mushrooms, and some kind of grain.

If I could pick one image that felt like my entire childhood, it would be those jars—filled with staples.

Flowers. My mother is nuts about flowers. She loves having them near her. She teaches children about them: "Loolie, look at the curve of this stem . . . Isn't it lovely? . . . Can you imagine something is just . . . shaped like that?" She treats flowers with her best care, and often uses them as first responders. For my mother, flowers and what one does with them—gardening, pruning, arranging, sending—are what it means to be civilized. If one of her kids' friends comes for the night, or if the Queen of England herself were to arrive, there would be a small vase on a chest or bedside table in their bedroom. If it is early in the summer, lush peonies. (My mother adores peonies because what is not to adore about a peony?, but also because it is the first flower my father gave her. He gave her a single peony on their first date; he bought it on Madison and Seventy-eighth Street, but didn't know its name.) Later, in August, she'll go for tangled sweet peas. In the fall, it could be delphiniums. And if it is Christmastime, as it was when I came home with the boys that gloomy December five years ago, there will be holly and little white roses by your bed. Those, bunched together in a glass vase, were what I noticed first when I brought my bags into my old room.

The boys, as if they were detectives entering a crime scene, poked around each room of the apartment, looking for the things that would be familiar: the Lunéville porcelain lion in the middle of the large, low, round wooden coffee table; the corner sofa whose cushions could be made into castles in the dark-red dining room; my brother's and my childhood copy of

Goodnight Moon in the little maid's room off the kitchen, where the boys would be sleeping that night (and almost every night for the next two years). They thought they were coming to their grandparents' home for Christmas, something we had done as a family every year since they were born; they didn't understand that we were going to *stay*.

All that was required of me that first evening was to go through the motions. Rub washcloths over little backs, locate the right stuffed animal, tuck in, sing lullabies. These routines felt comfortingly rote, but with an ache—the dull ache of doing it alone, knowing that no one would soon be coming home from the office to pitch in, to share. I could hardly look down at the boys' bewildered faces peering up at me from the single twin bed (the crib wouldn't be there until their father could drive it from Ohio). Thank God they had each other, I thought.

Once they were quiet, at my mother's urging, I took a bath. As the water rumbled, and my body relaxed against the old porcelain, I still was thinking: *Crikey*.

Now what? What on God's green earth was I going to do? Somehow, when someone is leaving you, everything feels so moment-to-moment. Well, your life as you knew it *is* hanging in the balance. You are like a surgeon trying to save this poor soul's life on the table—and the bitch of it is, you haven't been training for ten years to do this surgery. So you're in a mad rush to figure out how. And why and because of whom. You? Him? *Her?* And you are doing this surgery while desperately taking care of children whom you are watching like a hawk to see if there are any effects.

I had to get my shit together. I had to get my life back on track—and quickly, because my parents, well, it just wasn't their job to feed and shelter me forever and to feed and shelter the next generation forever, was it? They couldn't handle all of us in their apartment-sized space for very long, could they? Maybe we *would* always live together, I mused for a second. No. *Get it together, Isabel. Deal with this mess you made.*

But he left me.

I got out of the bath thinking, *Life isn't fair and it's hard, but what else is new?* I looked in the mirror with the green tile that had always been there, behind me in the reflection. I remembered soaping up those tiles with my brother, Andrew, while we took a bath when we were children. We thought it was fun to pretend we were washing windows. The suds got whiter and smoother as we moved them around with our little hands. I remembered checking to see if my headband was in place in that mirror the morning I graduated from high school. And I remembered leaning against that cool, milky green tile, watching my bridesmaids put mascara on the day I was married to Josiah.

• • •

Usually while cooking something that didn't need all that much attention—while browning meat or peeling potatoes, say—my mother every so often would tell me the story about Julia Child and her spun-sugar basket. On one episode of Julia Child's famous and beloved television show, she was demonstrating how to drizzle and spin hot sugar around and around on itself until eventually you had a sap-colored, delicate, bird's nest–like edible basket. All this spinning requires patience, skill, dedication. On the show, Julia spins and spins, building up the gossamer threads until eventually her masterpiece is complete. When she holds it up so the camera can get every angle, the basket drops and crashes to the ground. As my mother tells it (in her Julia Child impersonation that really just sounds like my mother), Mrs. Child briefly glances at the splendid mess on the floor, looks directly into the camera, and announces that the only thing to do at a point like this is to start again. She turns the stove back on and begins measuring sugar.

My beautiful sugar basket that I had put all my eggs into had crashed. I had to clean it up and start again.

In a situation like the one I was in, there's a big temptation never to examine what really happened, never to explore how the disaster came to be, because, socially at least, the crutch answer "My husband left me" can almost always get you off the hook for whatever relationship crimes you may also have committed. How could it be true that there was no work for me to do, no dark passages to investigate? I mean, who wants to go down a dark passage? But it struck me then, soaking in the tub, in the aroma of Florissa oil, that this broken sugar basket of a marriage had to be my fault, too. Part of getting my life together would be an investigation. I wanted to become a better person. I wanted to grow. I wanted to be married again and I wanted to be married for a much longer time than the six years that had just ended.

I was going to have to fully understand my recent history, and take advantage of the odd but perhaps instructive circumstance of living with both my parents and my children;

seeing myself simultaneously as a daughter and a mother was like looking in one of those infinity mirrors. I had a roof over my head and perhaps, if I did it right, the tools to start again. Still, my situation was weird and sad. I had not lived in Apartment 7A, my parents' home, for almost twenty years. My siblings (my brother Andrew and my two older half-brothers, David and Douglas) had all grown up and moved on. Even my room had moved on. There were no old ballet slippers or Grateful Dead posters left as reminders that this had once been a place I belonged. My mother had recently converted the room into an office for herself, and even though she had now moved the things she needed for her job as a consultant back into her bedroom, and even though she'd tried to make my old room nice for me by arranging a beautifully made bed, a small TV, a table (with the holly and little white roses in a sweet vase), and a chest of drawers for the boys, the room still felt like what it was supposed to be, her office. It was going to be unnatural for me and the boys to live here. I felt, at first, that we belonged somewhere else. I missed my husband and I worried that the children were in jeopardy without him. Even with the best intentions for plan B, I was lost.

But there were flowers.

chapter 3

The morning after my little boys and I tumbled into my parents' apartment for who knew how long, it was December 17, my wedding anniversary.

The kids sat on my bedroom floor and pulled clothes out of our still-packed duffel bags (if I could have, like a snake, I would have shed each item of clothing and started again). I took out the one file I had brought with all of our important documents in it. In my old life I had proper file cabinets that held years of old tax forms, birth certificates, and research info for endless projects, but when everything changed, I took only what was necessary to get me started in a new life. That turned out to be one folder full. In that folder were birth certificates, the children's medical records, a separation agreement that had only been drawn up three weeks before, my final paycheck from adjunct teaching at Oberlin College. And a recipe or two.

I took the separation agreement out of my everything-that's-important-in-life folder and folded the document awkwardly to fit it in my month-at-a-glance. I didn't know where to make the crease. I wasn't sure you should fold such a pronouncement, and thought maybe I should ask my mother for an 8″× 10″ envelope, something I knew she would have (along with paper clips, Wite-Out, and sewing kits with many different colored threads), but I thought better of asking my mother for office supplies that morning. This was my deal.

I was going to need a New York State driver's license to establish residency now so that I would qualify to take over the lease on my parents' rent-controlled apartment when they retired and moved to Maine at some point in the future. That apartment might be the only way I could afford to live in Manhattan as a single mother. And I thought that if I accomplished something practical and necessary on this day, it would distract me from the fact that exactly six years before, I had been hanging the wrinkles out of the long tulle veil.

I rode the subway to Penn Station and waited with the rest of New York to adjust my license at the License Express office. Then I proceeded to the Chase bank with my new license to open a bank account. I purposely had not deposited my last paycheck from teaching acting at Oberlin in our joint checking account (a move I felt guilty about, as if I were withholding something from Josiah that we had planned to share), but once it became clear that he was really leaving, I tried to be savvy and prepare for what was ahead. I hoped the check for $524, or something like that, would eventually be joined by the proceeds from the sale of our house, but until then it was enough to get me in at Chase.

Mrs. Bird, a refined, thin-wristed (I stared at her cuff links while she typed) black woman in her sixties, was kind to me as she looked over the separation agreement. I wondered if she noticed that I had been married on that very day six years earlier.

"You moved from Ohio, I see?"

"Yes. My husband left me," I said plainly. She didn't look up, but as happened with other people, it seemed that she understood; she made it very easy for me to set up a checking account with only my maiden name on it.

I came home to 275, which is the address of my parents' apartment building ("275" is what we always called it), like a gal who had just been stomping the pavement for a job. I had all of my new account information and a temporary driver's license under my arm, as if they were the classified section of the paper with red circles around promising-looking opportunities.

Wallace was out in the park with my dad. My mother was sitting on the window bench watching James playing next to the Christmas tree.

"Success? Was there a horrible line?" she said, referring to the License Express office.

"I got everything done," I said and picked up James.

"Not easy," she said. She wasn't talking about the lines.

"No." To prevent the tears from welling up, I nuzzled into my boy's neck, making him giggle a little.

"Well, well done, Loola," my mother said. Then she got up and walked purposefully toward the kitchen where the things she knew would help—grilled cheese on Pepperidge Farm bread, her cabbage soup, and Mallomars—could be found.

Next, I had to get a doctor for the children. What if they got sick? My friend Lisa told me to go to hers, Dr. Som, who was one of those rock-star Upper West Side pediatricians who took insurance. You would be surprised, but lots of pediatricians in New York don't. Josiah's good medical plan was one of the things we had going for us. Nervous, like a teenager calling another teenager, that this doctor wouldn't have space in his practice, I took a cleansing breath before I called to ask for an appointment. I worried that the receptionist would be able to tell through the telephone that I wasn't a secure, properly married New York mother, but a single mother. Just the fact that I was looking for a pediatrician for my two- and four-year-old boys made me feel bad because most *normal* people have had the same pediatrician since the first well-baby visit in the hospital. The doctor *knows* the children, can hear a different cough, is trusted by *the whole family*. We didn't have that, but we did get an appointment, so on a cold day I dressed us all up and headed out to meet Dr. Som.

As we'd waited outside our building for the M10 bus that would take us near the doctor, Sheila, a downstairs neighbor whom I had known since I was ten, was getting out of her taxi. She was slight, Jewish, and had a big friendly smile.

When I was about thirteen, my parents had received a small orange tree as thanks for a dinner from a fancy friend. My brother and I were elated by the tree; it looked exactly like every fantasy one might have about California. Cool people have orange trees in their apartments in New York City; rock stars. My mother, however, was undone by it.

"My goodness," she exclaimed, reeling from the sight of it.

"Where on earth are we going to put it?" She looked at it as if it were a python.

"In the living room!" we begged. I had this feeling that tree was not long for Apartment 7A. She walked around it in her coat, holding her briefcase and a bag of groceries. "Well, I just don't know the first thing about taking care of an orange tree . . . He"—she was referring to the tree—"is not going to like it in this climate."

By the morning the tree was gone. My parents had decided to give it to Sheila and Rog, who lived just below us on the sixth floor. They had modern taste and a different view of the world, a view from which orange trees were not so shocking. They loved it for a long time.

Anyway, I'm sure Sheila had heard what had happened to me and knew why I was moving back into the building and onto the seventh floor, but I had not seen her yet. When she got out of her cab, and after she had taken in the scene of my scruffy kids swinging around and around the awning poles like little Gene Kellys in *Singin' in the Rain*, she pointed her beautifully manicured finger at me and said in an attractive New York accent, "You know what you need?" She paused briefly, but I knew not to answer. "You need three pounds. And a husband."

•   •   •

Oh, I didn't want to live in Manhattan, not really, it's so . . . loony. Just getting out of a taxi with two little kids is ridiculous in Manhattan. You are trying to pay the twenty-seven dollars you owe to the cabbie for the ten minutes you were in his car, while tugging madly on the stroller that is now stuck under the seat. The toddler is asleep in your lap like a ten-ton sack of flour, and the four-year-old has already scampered out on the curb, having been swerved around by a bike messenger—"Wait, sweetheart! Don't move! Stay on the sidewalk! Mom's almost done here!" And then you forget the bag of groceries or the phone has slid out of your coat pocket, never to be seen again.

But Manhattan was where I was, and I had to grow where I was planted. (Or maybe gain three pounds and get a new husband.)

In the doctor's office, I had to face the music right away. Upon entry I was asked everyone's name. For the first time in their lives, the children didn't have the same last name as I did; as of two weeks before, I had been walking around calling myself Isabel Robinson. Now, of course there are millions of mothers who don't share the same last name as their children, but the fact that I no longer did didn't make me feel like a feminist, it made me feel like a divorced person.

"Yes, right, I am Gillies, they are Robinson. Sorry—confusing," I whispered so the kids wouldn't hear me.

Waiting for the famous Dr. Som in the examining room, I glided my hand up and down the tiny spine and smooth back of my not-yet-two-year-old and stroked the older one's hair, pulling the robe over and over again back onto his shoulders. Their white underpants and soft feet wrinkled the crinkly paper that covered the bench we were all sitting on, and their curious hands reached for cold medical instruments. It took a long time, so I gave the little one a tiny paper cup to play with and attempted to read them a frayed old children's book, not caring that most of the pages were ripped out.

While the doctor looked in their ears and eyes, the boys sucked their thumbs.

"They both suck their thumbs?" he asked in interest.

"Yes, they always have. I think it soothes them," I said, wondering if he thought I was a bad mother.

"Oh, it's all right," he said, casually getting out his mallet to bonk their knees.

I felt that I needed to confess to the doctor that we were in a predicament. I thought it would be important for him to know, if he was going to be our trusted pediatrician. The way he said it was all right that they sucked their thumbs made me think that he already knew.

"Doctor," I said as he was getting ready to leave the room, as the boys were fumbling with clothes. "We have moved back to New York because their dad and I are—" I mimed getting divorced like I was in a bad sitcom. I mimed the ring flying off my finger and sort of crossed my eyes and stuck my tongue out of the side of my mouth like I had just gotten hanged. I needed him to take care of me, too.

"I see. Well, you have fine boys there. Don't try and stop them from sucking their thumbs, not now," he said, lifting his unruly eyebrows, and he left the room.

Those were my accomplishments: a driver's license, a bank balance of $524, and a pediatrician for my children. You cannot imagine how satisfying (even if it is a little galling because you so recently had already had the bank account, driver's license, et cetera) it is to get those things done. However, getting them done did not leave me with much energy for other domestic efforts. I did cook bacon every morning because I thought the smell would trick the boys into thinking they weren't from a broken home, but 85 percent of my instinct to nest fizzled when I moved back into 275.

I felt adolescent. I had only enough mental and financial capability to put up a Red Hot Chili Peppers poster, nothing near the wherewithal required to put up a roll of wallpaper (something I'd been able to do in Ohio). I did go with the boys to Staples and buy a corkboard, and I handwrote and tacked up on this corkboard a list of *important numbers*. I thought this was being responsible (the need for me to maintain a modicum of propriety was strong, although sometimes it felt like a losing battle). But the corkboard looked pathetic, because not only did I not have a printer, but I could only conjure up two numbers: Dr. Som and Josiah. My old list, in Ohio, had been so hearty and impressive. It had many doctors and handymen, office numbers, garbage pickup times, school numbers, neighbors, vets, nearest hospitals. I even had numbers in other states, like Josiah's first son Ian's school in Dallas, and Ian's mother and stepfather's work numbers. I was in charge, official; I had super-mom style. There were so many people to reach if we were in need, so many contacts, so many connections. But now that I really was in need I could only think up two. Of course, my parents were there with their bulging 1970s rolodexes-worth of connections. (My mother did make a huge effort to join the computer age and has endless and meticulous databases on her PC, but she used to have the most marvelous round rolodexes with hundreds of manila cards jammed in alphabetically. Some of the addresses and numbers were typed using an actual typewriter, either by my mother or by Marion, her longtime secretary at the foundation where she worked, but others were written or updated in my mother's bizarre, chic, and illegible-to-anyone-not-intimately-close-to-her handwriting, which is vertical and narrow so it looks like a bunch of paper clips mushed together.) To beef up my bulletin board list, I looked in the telephone book and added the numbers for poison control, the local police department, and all of Wallace and James's paternal grandparents, though it was not like they could do anything in an emergency, as they lived miles away in different states.

I wanted to add pictures of my friends, but initially resisted the urge because I feared it would resemble my wall in high school. I already felt close to re-watching every John Hughes movie ever made; a big photo montage on my wall would reveal for certain that I had lost my standing as a proper lady-of-the-house, that I had reverted to bubble letters. But the cork looked so empty, so stark, and I wasn't the lady of the house, my mother was, so I tacked up pictures of my friends and their kids. I even did rip out a black-and-white photo of the Red Hot Chili Peppers that I found in *Rolling Stone*. It was from an article promoting their new album. All the songs were about beginnings, rejuvenation, new love. Most of the guys were just married or remarried, and some had babies. That band went through hell and came out the other side, so I tacked up their photo right alongside my skimpy list. You have to start somewhere, even if it's with Anthony Kiedis.

chapter 4

This feels a little weird to write because I'm sure it's the Drama Mama in me that makes me feel this way, but when your husband or wife leaves you, it's exciting. It's also horrible and frightening and so sad, but I have to admit, and hindsight might be helping me admit this a bit, it's exciting. It's not exciting like going on a trip somewhere you have never been, it's exciting like getting in trouble. Nobody wants a storm, but I guess sometimes people need them and feel invigorated by the darkness and uncertainty. You are in the middle of a spectacle, a big, sexy, dark crisis. People call you all the time because you very well may be on the edge of something. For a time, you get to drink one more glass of wine than you should and cry at the drop of a hat. You are allowed to feel pitiful and eat junk food, because let's face it, when the ship is going down, why not have an éclair?

And because your old life isn't quite over yet, but you know it will be soon, it's safe to indulge in tiny moments of fantasizing about what your future could hold. When the daydreams don't crush you (destitution, depressed children, loneliness), they excite you. (You can fantasize that you marry Prince Harry. Why not? You are certainly older than he is and a commoner, but you are both single. Stranger things have surely happened.) Those fantasy moments are short-lived, and really what you do a lot in the middle of the night is miss your spouse.

Among the many sad losses in my life just then was that I was losing my husband as a friend. It wouldn't stay that way forever, we are friends now, but there is a clear arena for ex-spouses, and we weren't there yet, it was too soon. For the time being, losing the title of wife left me feeling unsure of exactly who I was (I loved my eggs being in that wife basket). We spoke, but it was shrouded in uncertainty. It was all a mess. Our oasis was the boys: A discussion about a loose tooth or bad dream went smoothly, and felt free and connected, but when we exhausted the topic, that was it, he didn't want to chat or linger. And if I am really honest, the loose tooth conversations, at first, had a hint of, See, he's losing teeth and *you are missing it!*

Everything we were together was being redefined by the hour. The panicky feeling I had wasn't only guilt, bills, and unanswered questions, it was that feeling of losing a connection. Being left with life, all alone. I loathe feeling left out. Sometimes when being left alone made me mad, instead of letting Josiah have it, I would e-mail or call Sylvia. Sylvia was who Josiah was leaving me for. There was a lot of talk that that wasn't actually the case—he had argued that the marriage was over for a ton of reasons besides her—but she was one young, beautiful reason.

Once, I impulsively called her at her office. (My impulsivity was something I was starting to take a look at during this time; it was dawning on me that that kind of behavior might be problematic. I had always thought that being impulsive was sort of chic—flying on impulse to San Francisco to see an English boy playing saxophone in a band, going to the movies in the morning—but moments like the upcoming one were teaching me that restraint might be more attractive than I'd previously imagined.) Anyway, I called from that desk my mother had designed for herself. Even though I was probably in my pajamas looking out on the frumpy-looking Upper West Side in winter, the shape of the desk and the rolling chair made me feel like I was Gordon Gekko. They gave me a false sense of power.

"I would never get in the way of a reconciliation between you and Josiah," Sylvia said, smooth as silk. This woman, whom I respect a lot these days, is über-composed. A Jedi.

"Oh, yeah," I said, gearing up for a zinger. "Are you fucking him?"

Silence.

Beat, beat, beat.

"Because if you are, that is seriously getting in the way of reconciliation."

We hung up simultaneously.

•   •   •

The thing was, I wasn't really mad at either of them. I was beyond that. I was frustrated, and I felt like I lived in the Twilight Zone or was on acid. Change can feel psychedelic.

How could I rebuild in New York? New York is complicated and expensive, and it seemed impossible that I would be able to live even one day there with any kind of success, much less build a life, even though I was born and raised there. But you can rebuild, because nothing is impossible, especially in New York City. It is a never-ending construction site. It's actually a great place to start again. There are a million choices in New York City. Choices are good, even small ones; make them, and they keep you moving forward. Be decisive.

I did not have a choice, though, of reuniting with Josiah; that was where *he* was being very decisive. He never wanted me back. However, one evening right at the beginning of my new life, I got confused.

I had put the boys to bed at 7:00, which may seem early, but it had already been dark for two hours, and for them, the days were long. It's exhausting to learn to wait for elevators and the walk sign (two things they didn't have in Ohio). It's exhausting to watch your mother make a million phone calls (lawyer, real estate people, passport offices, manager, friends) when all you want her to do is play with you on the floor. And it's exhausting to be adjusting to something constantly, as my boys were, even to volume and texture. "Mama, this place is made of iron," Wallace said of his new city.

Most little children fight bedtime; I think it's because their day has been childlike and fun. When the day ended, my boys looked thankful. Bedtime was one story and four of the same lullabies in the same order:

"You Can Close Your Eyes" (James Taylor)
"Here Comes the Sun" (Beatles)
"April Come She Will" (Paul Simon)
"Brahms' Lullaby" (Brahms)

There was a two-foot space between the boys as they slept. If they reached out, they could hold hands, and sometimes you could catch them doing just that. The wee space was a blessing for the three of us. They had just fallen and didn't know how badly it was going to hurt yet. When a child falls, my instinct, once I get over the surprise of the spill and give them a moment, is to hold them tight, confine them quickly. The small, simple space of the room felt safe, womblike. At night, I would sit in there, and perhaps the only comfort for any of us was that we were close together.

After I finished singing, they would put their thumbs in their mouths and watch me as I put my hands over my head and shooed away everything scary toward the window, as if there were smoky air above us. *Shhh Shhh Shhh Shhh*. It sounded like someone threshing wheat. This was a new ritual since we had come to New York, and they counted on it every night. A nuzzle for both of them and I was free to collapse and have a glass of wine. (Some mothers have a glass of wine during the wind-down because it takes the edge off; I save it for when I am really done. Like a reward, I guess, but also like the glass of water the volunteer hands the marathoners at the end of the race. I guess there are a ton of people who don't even drink, but I am not one of them.)

My mother was at the stove giving something a taste.

"Can I help?" I mouthed. (Ever since the boys and I had moved in, 70 percent of the talking my mother and I did in the kitchen had to be in whispers. Someone was almost always sleeping right next door.) She shook her head no, thankfully. Cooking, something I am usually passionate about and love to do, seemed like a burden. (In fact, my mother recently told me that early on, when I first got back from Ohio, I burst into tears when she started to measure the rice for dinner. The two things in the world that I really couldn't cook were rice and coffee, so Josiah always cooked the rice. Happily, I have since learned how to make a good cup of coffee, though I still can't cook rice.) I gingerly walked back to "my room," sat at the desk my mother had designed for herself, took a deep breath, and checked my e-mail. There was one from Josiah.

It had an attachment, but no words. I opened it and there were about twenty-five pictures of pelicans. I love pelicans. I really love them. I love how big they are, that they fly usually in pairs, and that if there are more than a pair, they always fly in formation. They are symbols of motherhood and of Jesus, and at the end of *Jurassic Park*, Spielberg closes the movie with an image of one, signaling that they are the living descendants of dinosaurs on earth. I have always loved them and Josiah knew it. When I would go with him to his stepmother's family's house in North Carolina, I was able to see them in the wild, flying along the beach like patrollers. Steady, big, confident.

I scrolled down through picture after picture of those beautiful birds and started trembling. It was a love letter! It was his way of saying he had made a mistake and he wanted me back. I smiled a big wide smile and got all the hope in the world that this was my cue to pack up our things from the strange, bizarro world of living with my parents and my children in the same apartment in an intimidating city and get the hell back home where I belonged, to a town with three stoplights and a real five-and-dime, my brick house, my job in the drama department, to my husband who understood me. The father of my sleeping boys was maybe the only person on earth who knew how much I loved pelicans. He was saying he was sorry for leaving me for another woman and asking my forgiveness. Get it, pelicans? Jesus?

I was just waiting, anticipating. How would he ask me? Would he just blurt it out? Maybe he would say something like, "Come home. I'm sorry. I'm a stupid idiot and I would do anything in the world if you would come back." Or would we chat for a little while about the boys and our life, mistakes and regrets? It would be unspoken, and the next day I would make plane reservations, tell my parents they could change their lives back, as we would be going home.

I ate dinner with my parents, did the dishes, opted out of seeing what was on PBS with bowls of vanilla ice cream and chocolate sauce, went into my room and closed the door.

I climbed into bed with the telephone and called Josiah.

"Hello?" He sounded surprised that the phone had rung at 9:45 p.m.

"Hi, it's me," I cooed.

"Is everything all right with the boys?" he worried.

"Yeah, yeah, they're fine. Sleeping."

I was lying that they were fine. They really were not. James was all right because he was so little, but Wallace was a wreck. Most of the time he would sit in a corner, one thumb in his mouth, the other over his eyes. If he had two other hands, they would be over his ears. No, he was not all right; he felt all of it more than anyone.

But I didn't get into that at all with Josiah because this was the call that was about to return everything to normal.

"Oh, good," he said. "What's up?"

"Umm, well, I got your e-mail," I said.

"What e-mail?" he said plainly.

This was not good.

"All those pelicans?" I said.

"Did the boys like them?" he asked. I could feel my chest constrict and suddenly, without being able to stop, I started to cry.

He was silent.

"But they were pelicans."

"Isabel, I'm sorry, I thought the boys would like them," he said.

"Yeah, well, I didn't show them to the boys because I thought they were for me." I wiped my tears with my arm and felt stupid and like he was fucking with me.

"Oh, I wasn't thinking. I'm sorry. No, they were for the boys," he said quietly.

"Well, next time you should fucking think about what you are sending me, Josiah."

"Okay. Again, I'm sorry."

We were both quiet.

"Okay," he said. "I'll call tomorrow to say hello to the boys," ending the phone call.

"Okay," I said.

And we hung up. He never confused me again.

It doesn't go away, the importance you put on one single person, the value that he had for you, the assumption that you would lie beside him forever; the hope you had for your union is so great that the loss of it doesn't go away. To move forward you have to dig an internal grave and intentionally put that hope to rest. People will try to help you, but you must do it yourself. You bury it like a body in the earth and pray that whatever it was for you will give life to something else—like a tree—and hope that with every year that new life will become bigger, stronger, and more beautiful. But that loss doesn't ever go away, not entirely.

Josiah has since sent the boys many pictures of animals on my computer, but they always have a message attached: For the boys.

chapter 5

Wallace had to go to nursery school.
        I am many things, but a homeschooler is not one
of them. Getting your child into school at age 2.9 in New York
is no joke. It's like a combination of trying to get into the best,
most happening restaurant and MIT. Most of the nursery
schools are private and the application process takes nine
months (that is, if you didn't start courting a school when the
child was born). Even if the local public school has a pre-K,
and most do not, there is a wait list as long as Manhattan Island (eleven miles). You would have had to get going with that
process months and months in advance.

I knew all this about the schools in New York City, and it
was one of the reasons I had been so happy to be living in a
small college town where all you have to do is show up with
your little guy in August and say, "This is Wallace and he'll be
starting in the fall." Not in NYC, no.

Almost the minute the word "separate" started to fly around
my life, I started worrying about where Wallace would land

preschool-wise. From my kitchen in Oberlin, I began making calls to see if by any chance there was a spot open somewhere. The first five people I spoke to at a variety of preschools sort of paused, as a way of saying, "Are you kidding me?", then told me flat out that there was no room at the inn, not this year and probably not the next year either, as it was already November and the application process started in September. I was expecting this kind of response to my situation, so each conversation felt more like a head-scratcher than a big disappointment.

My mother was also on the case in New York. She spoke to a friend, who told her about this thirty-year-old Montessori school on the Upper West Side not that far from where my parents lived. It was the first school in the United States to close its doors to protest the Vietnam War—even before Harvard. A bunch of mothers had started this school in the Sixties, and it had the reputation of being a nurturing, well-run, funky place where teachers came from all over the world. My mother had even walked over to look at the doorway, at the kids going in and out. The motto was "A Place to Begin." Thinking we all needed a place to begin, I took a deep breath and made the "Hail Mary" call. Becky, whom I always think of now as the Angel of New York, answered the phone.

"West Side Montessori," she said in a heavy New York accent. (And she said "West Side" in a lower tone that got higher as she said "Montessori.")

"Hi. My name is Isabel Gillies, and, well, I'm calling from Ohio, because—" Then I decided just to be truthful, not dramatic, but honest about why I needed what I needed. I did this more because I didn't want to come across as disorganized than because I wanted a total stranger to know my personal business.

"Anyway, I was wondering if there was any chance that I could still apply for my boy for the fall?" Hopeful but ready.

There was a different kind of pause, then, than the are-you-kidding-me pause.

"What about January?" she said on the down-low, like a good fishmonger who knows about something in the back that the general public doesn't know about.

"Uh, well, January would be great," I said, almost in a whisper, not really believing what I was hearing.

"Just between you and me, twins left."

After falling all over myself in gratitude, even though I wasn't wholly sure at that point just *how* grateful I should have been or what I was getting into, I started writing an essay about Wallace to send off to New York.

There was a spot, *a* spot, and we had to go to an interview to get it. It sounds a little crazy to be a little crazy about a spot in school for a four-year-old where all they do is count beans and sing, but in New York, and I'm sure a lot of other places in the country, this stuff keeps people up at night.

We scheduled the interview. The boys and I moved to New York. And on January 16, Wallace and I made our first journey to Ninety-fourth Street and West End Avenue. As we approached, I noticed other people my age pushing strollers or holding the hands of little ones, all anxiously heading in the same direction, like we were sperm gunning for the same egg. This wasn't just an interview for my kid, this was an interview day for all the spots for the next September and for the one we wanted. There were about sixty children going on their "classroom visits." A cattle call of sorts.

One shot and then a judgment? It was like the Olympics, but for my baby. Suddenly, I felt like I was wearing the wrong thing and I was applying at the wrong time, feeling the way I'd felt in the pediatrician's office. If I were a *normal* mother, I wouldn't be trying to cram my kid into school at the eleventh hour; I would have started angling to get a school spot for Wallace when he was eight months old, like all the *normal* mothers did.

We climbed the four flights of stairs in the old townhouse and entered room 4W. Montessori classrooms have a lightness. Maria Montessori believed that children should and are quite capable of learning their own way through the world, guided gently, but not directed. They should accomplish tasks by themselves. They should be given appropriate responsibility to do their "work" (not play), do up their own buttons, take care of their possessions, make peace, and manage their own friendships and feelings. For instance, in the morning it is one kid's job to serve the snack for the day—to prepare the food, to figure out the portions (twenty kids, forty apple slices, two each), and to write the message to the other children about how much each can have (if you can't write yet, you can draw the apples). Montessori classrooms have mixed ages, so if you need help from an older child with different skills than you have, you know who they are and how to find them. By the end of the year it's clear who can help you with what. You need help to write, go to Sophia; need to know about the stars, Andrew; need help making peace with a pal, Frederick.

And they communicate through messages:

"Daniel, Toby has a message for you," says the calm, maybe Tibetan or French Montessori teacher.

Toby: "Daniel Breecher [the children all know and use each other's entire names], your body is too close to mine and I DON'T LIKE IT." (Kids love telling another kid they don't like something; with feeling.)

No holiday is celebrated, not Halloween or Hanukkah. On a kid's birthday there are no cupcakes or candles, but the birthday person brings in a picture of themselves from every year that they have been alive and gets to "walk around the sun."

At the interview, children and teachers, with all their Montessori mojo, muddled around the classroom, doing puzzles and measuring sand, while the parents anxiously (but pretending not to be in the slightest) sat on the stairs and watched.

Wallace walked over to an easel, picked up a crayon, and started to draw. He stood very straight and made big sweeping motions with his arms. He drew circles and used color, and at the end looked up at the young man who was observing him and said, "It's the weather."

He made one concerted effort for us, and not only was it a beautiful one, but it was of the sun and a blue sky. I knew his world wasn't very sunny. I knew he probably wanted to crawl on my lap, suck his thumb, and stare into the mirror to the side of the stairs; he more than likely wanted to draw a tempest, but he didn't. He was brave, and he must have felt safe in there.

A couple of days later we got a call from the admissions director that he could come to school when they started up again in a few weeks. And a few weeks after that, I even got financial aid.

chapter 6

Nobody had had a hard time identifying that Josiah was deeply involved with Sylvia but me. I was pretty much the only idiot in the room continually saying the marriage "just didn't work out and he just didn't want to be married to me." I shared this belief with my best friend, Bess. We were operating under the assumption that Josiah and I were simply having a modern parting of ways. Other than Bess and I, everyone already suspected that nothing modern at all was going on; Josiah was just old-fashioned leaving his wife (me) for another woman. Then, on a frigid day in February, Josiah called to tell me that Sylvia and he were indeed a couple and were living together. He wouldn't have broken that news to me unless it was set in stone. They might as well have been married at that point. This was the end of Josiah and me for real, and for the next two weeks, I went mad.

Think Ophelia and her herbs, Jessica Lange in *Frances*. Insanity. This was not ancient anger from some quirky parenting glitch in my upbringing that any shrink could work out eventually, this was legit, I've-been-fucked-over, red-hot rage.

I left the boys with my flabbergasted parents, called Bess, and flew to her apartment.

Her kids were napping, so imagine this scene in muted hysteria. Bess opened the door. She was beside herself. Stamping in slow motion so as not to wake her boys, and with her fist pounding up in the air, she whispered, "Okay! Okay. So now we know. Goddamn it!"

I beelined into her bathroom and threw up. When I came out, she was still in the hallway. She hugged me. Then I sobbed. When I finished (by this point I was so used to sobbing, it was no big deal to either of us), she waved toward the kitchen, and I knew what that meant: "The kettle is on, let's make the tea."

With two oversized mugs of Lady Grey in our hands, we curled into her sofa. (Thank God for napping children.)

"Well, Izzle, at least you know."

"I know, but it's just so frat boy, right? Leaving the wife and kids for the hot chick? It's so the-guy-that-went-to-Boston-College-and-sits-at-the-bar. I can't get over it."

"It's despicable," she said tentatively; she knew very well I had little tolerance for anyone who spoke badly about my boys' father, even at that moment.

"I know," I said. "I just can't believe it. I can't believe her!" And it was as if just by saying the word "her" something clicked in me. I was the "wronged" woman and she was the "other" woman. There was a tried-and-true formula there that I could plug into. I had been trying to avoid clichés, but now that he had put the biggest cliché in the world on a platter before me, I was going to dig in.

In the taxi going back to feed the boys, I wasn't Isabel the meek, fallen one anymore; I was powerful—like Alex Forrest, the 1980s lunatic from the movie *Fatal Attraction*. Of course, when I got home my mother had already fed dinner to the boys. She was already herding them toward the tub when I burst open the front door. I was wearing a fuchsia poncho that my friend Sasha had handed down to me along with two suitcases filled with her old clothes. She has great clothes and I wore her hand-me-downs like a little sister for the next two years.

The poncho added to my woman-on-the-verge-of-a-nervous-breakdown vibe. My mother and father, each holding a boy's hand, looked at me, wide-eyed. I looked at them right back. I was officially a crazy person. If they had ever been fuzzy about the meaning behind the saying, "Hell hath no fury like a woman scorned," they were about to get a vivid picture.

I started out by e-mailing most of the Oberlin English department a group e-mail. In my note I revealed the relationship my husband was having with their other colleague. I called her a "cold, steel-hearted wolf," and I damned them all to hell for being blasé and just going with the flow of an extramarital affair being conducted in "our" small community instead of getting to work sewing a lot of scarlet "A"s. (Now that I am older and have seen more Sodom and Gomorrah situations infiltrate communities, I realize that people tend to go with the flow of affairs much more than you would think.)

Then I ranted into the answering machines of everyone I

knew in Oberlin, but mostly into Josiah's, crying, hysterical, yelling, and then finally slamming the phone down into its cradle. For some reason Josiah tended not to pick up the phone much those days. I wanted desperately to call Sylvia's mother, but never could find the number, not in all my cuckoo-loony 411 calls to Vermont, where I suspected she lived.

I curled up on the floor in agony, wandered around looking like a wreck, obsessively Googled Sylvia, and watched Woody Allen movies on cable and tried to intellectualize my feelings the way Diane Keaton's characters were so good at doing. I wore the same jeans for days on end, took Ambien to get to sleep, and found very little pleasure in anything. I knew, in the back of my mind, that I was playing with fire. I knew my children were not so young that they wouldn't feel this, irreparably, soon. Then one day I was in the kitchen with four-year-old Wallace, who had fished an eggbeater out of a large kitchen utility drawer. He was always hauling around something odd like a drum, a toilet paper roll, or an eggplant, so the fact that he had a ball of string didn't faze me. He sat on the floor, lacing the string through all the spokes of the beater. When he had finished, he gave me the ball of string attached to it all and said, "Mama, I am going to wind the anger out of you."

And with that, my madness came to an end. I returned to just being sad.

The saddest I ever got was soon after Wallace's eggbeater plea. I had left our china in Ohio. But before I took off, I had put aside a few plates, platters, and vases that I felt were too pretty to give up. I had asked Josiah to send them to New York, and so he did.

They arrived in the early evening via UPS. There was something about the box that seemed ominous to me. It was worn-out looking, like it had traveled much farther than from Ohio. Josiah's handwriting on the top made me wince, and I regretted instantly that I had asked him to go to the trouble, because no plate was pretty enough to be worth the pain I would feel upon opening the box. I went into my mother's room and got a letter opener. I had never really liked walking into my parents' room when they were not there. It felt intrusive. But since I had moved back in, walking into their room was 100 percent worse, because it was their only refuge from us. Anyway, of course, my mother had a letter opener; it's the kind of tool that she lives for.

As I lifted the first items out, I knew just by the feel of them that they were broken, like a candy cane that gets crushed in its cellophane wrapper. Almost all of the china had been cracked or shattered during the trip. I don't think Josiah ever imagined anything would break during the journey, but he hadn't gotten a mover to professionally wrap the seven pieces to send to New York, and the paper he chose was too thin and almost nothing survived.

All of the smashed china happened to be wedding presents from his mother. She knew about good things, but she also paid attention to the subjects and details people were drawn to. If she gave you something, it was in the color you wore most, featured the animal you admired, or was useful for a hobby you took pleasure in. The broken china that I was holding in my hands had fragments of painted, swooping birds and twisting dragons on them. As a bride, I had imagined that I would use those precious, beautiful plates over and over again, at Thanksgivings and eighteenth birthdays. As I knelt down to collect all the broken pieces in the thin paper and head to the kitchen garbage pail, it felt like I was throwing away everything that is important about Thanksgiving and eighteenth birthdays, throwing away the evidence of a happy family.

part
II

chapter 7

Even with the financial aid at Wallace's school, the full knowledge that I wouldn't be moving back to Oberlin (you can think you've let go of something and find that you really haven't—that can go on for longer than you think) brought a spotlight to my desperate need to sell our house in Ohio and wake up my dormant acting career. It is stunning how much New York costs. I was living in a safety hammock. My parents were paying for the lighting bill and most of the food, and I was getting child support to help cover everything from co-pays at the doctor to rain boots; still, I needed an income.

And this house thing was downright depressing because we had just bought and renovated it, thinking it was the place we'd live in for the next twenty years. You don't exactly buy houses to flip 'em in small towns in Ohio. I would lose money, and even though I know money isn't everything (it's love, it's love, it's love), it sort of is when you have two little kids. And the house money, which came from my grandmother, was all I had.

The same guy who had sold it to us the year before would be selling it again. He was an older Ohio gentleman named Mr. Wells, who worked in real estate with his very nice wife. They were a duo. He would call me to give updates: "Someone is coming to see it again. I'm not sure they care that the wallpaper is new." I had put really pretty paper in that house, but apparently even the most charming Clarence House print does not add a lot of value. I kept saying, "Don't they care? That brown was discontinued!" Mr. Wells clearly felt terrible about the situation. I mean, just months before we had been exclaiming how perfect the house was for a young family, growing boys, Thanksgivings, ugh. Every time we spoke, we both got sad.

At least *they* were not going to live in it. That happens. I have a friend whose ex-husband and new wife lived in their family house after the divorce. It has been more than twenty years, but whenever she is there visiting (they have two children and a friendly relationship—a must-have, or at least something to seriously shoot for, if you have children), she looks at the roses crawling up the side of the house and thinks maybe a little wistfully, "I planted those."

Our house eventually did sell, and along with a check that would help me, I was left with a lot of wonderings. Would they love having dinner on the deck in the back? Would they notice how *many* fireflies there were out there? Would they think the yellow in the living room was the prettiest yellow they had ever seen? Would they read the paper on the window bench in the kitchen that was made for reading the paper on?

•   •   •

Before I went out to Ohio to start the new life of a professor's wife, I was the wife of Elliot Stabler (played by the steady and strong Chris Meloni), the lead detective on *Law & Order: Special Victims Unit*. When the job started I was twenty-eight, unmarried, a bit in the clouds, a decent actor, and lucky. Usually on *Law & Order* they don't bother with the lead characters' personal lives because the real star of the show is the crime. But this series was about *sex* crimes, and Dick Wolf, the creator, was not going to have an Irish Catholic male cop on the show talking about pedophiles without a nice wife and four small children at home (we now have five). I turned out to be that wife. I remember the audition as if it were yesterday. I had been on the original *Law & Order* (the mother ship) about a year before. I got to play a young, punky kid who kills a cop. It was a great episode, beautifully directed by Jace Alexander, and had a lot of wonderful New York stage actors in it playing lawyers and judges. I was executed at the end of the show, but before that I found God. The episode was based on the Tammy Faye Tucker story, and in case it isn't obvious, the part was an actor's dream. I was damn lucky to get it. (In twenty years as an actress, I probably auditioned about 7,500 times and got about 20 parts, and out of those only 5 were something to write home about.) I even got to confess my guilt to the incredible Sam Waterston on the stand: "That is *my* knife. I killed that cop." Man, it was fun.

Anyway, at my audition for Kathy Stabler, I had the murder show under my belt, and in addition to that, I had auditioned a number of times for *L&O* during the previous year. I was on that casting office's screen. From the time my manager called me about the audition (I was actually shopping for my wedding dress when he called), I knew that not only did I want the part badly, but if I played my cards right I just might get it. It was my time, and that was what I told Dick Wolf.

Josiah and I were supposed to go to Dallas to see his son, but because of the audition I didn't go. After reading the scene where my TV son's turtle gets killed in the disposal, I looked at Mr. Wolf and bravely said, "Mr. Wolf, I can play this part and I think you should give it to me. You see, I was supposed to go visit my future stepson in Texas, but because of this audition, I'm not, and he will probably need a ton of therapy to deal with it." I said all this half-smiling and almost wide-eyed. Who *on earth* did I think I was, talking to one of the most famous and powerful television producers of all time like that?

"I know what you mean about therapy," he said in his sort of 1940s gangster voice. "I'm going to be paying for it for my kids for the rest of my life!" He said all of that with a cackle and a twinkle, looking at his producing partner. Clearly, to create the most influential and beloved television series in history, you have to miss a couple of class plays.

I laughed nervously and pretended that I knew exactly what he was talking about.

"Yeah, well, I really would love the part," I said, as if I needed to say it. It was a part that changed my life.

Even though it was a great job to get, it wasn't a huge part. The family and I were basically there just to illustrate the parallels between home and work life for Chris Meloni's character. If he was handling the rape case of a six-year-old girl, he would personally struggle with it because of his own child, etc. In the first three *SVU* seasons, my character showed up in a handful of sweet but maybe uninspiring, underwritten scenes. As an actor, I was okay—serviceable, usually nervous. I remember one time I couldn't remember a particular line that I was saying while Chris was eating chicken. I messed up around ten times. I'll never forget the look on his face as the props person gave him yet another drumstick. I knew he was thinking, "Can you get it together and remember the damn line, you little spaz!?!" In order to get me out of my rut, the director of the episode made me run around the abandoned parking lot at the back of the studio in big circles. I think it was two in the morning.

My character was consistently bummed out about how little her husband was around, always in a huge tent of a housedress, and *always* stirring something on the stove. I wanted them to be happier than they were, and the rest of the country (mostly) wanted my husband and his partner, Olivia, to be together.

In real life, I got married, had two babies, got divorced and remarried all during my tenure on the show. When I moved to Ohio with Josiah, my part diminished greatly, although they did fly me back to NYC for one episode during the year and a half I was there. But by the time I moved back after my separation, the writers had my TV husband and me in marital crisis and headed for a divorce.

When I had called Ken, my longtime manager, from my front steps in Ohio to tell him I was divorcing and needed to get back to work, all he had to say was, "Good luck."

I remember clicking off the phone, staring onto the dead quiet of Elm Street in Ohio, and thinking, *Fuck.*

Ken wasn't wrong. Memories are short in TV and movie casting, and I had been gone for ages. I had to start from scratch, and starting from scratch as an actress at thirty-five is no easy task. Laughable, really.

One day while I was doing something very unglamorous, like watching the PBS kids' show *Franklin* in my room with the boys, the phone rang.

"Hey, it's Ken. So guess what? *SVU* wants to know if you are available to shoot in the next two weeks. I think you guys are divorcing," he said with no pulse.

"Oh, great. I'm divorcing on real life and on NBC, how cool," I said drolly back. "But *yes!* I am free. I am nothing but free."

Now, here's the thing: I had lost about twenty pounds. There is *nothing* a producer likes more than an actress who is thin as a rail. Thin = pretty in TV land, and America likes pretty. The scene I had in the episode was basically just standing next to Chris at our daughter's confirmation. I didn't say much, but they must have liked it because very soon after I got another phone call.

"Hey, it's Ken. So guess what? They want you back again. This time you are really divorcing," he said, and he sounded amused.

"Hey, man, I'll get divorced for the rest of my life as long as I get top of show!" (Top of show is a pay scale thing in TV.)

So I went back to New Jersey where the *SVU* studio was, but this time the scene was me asking my husband for clarity in our relationship. He hadn't signed the divorce papers and I wanted to know why.

Instead of staying in one of the stark dressing rooms that are used for characters like mine who don't come in all that often, I lay on the floor of the squad room. (Lying on the floor is a great way for your body to open up. Just try lying on the floor sometime, you almost immediately feel more vulnerable; you might even start to cry.) For once in all my years on the series, they'd put me in a pretty dress, so I lay on the floor in that, breathed, and imagined what it would be like if I could just have a moment to ask Josiah for clarity, for a real answer. What would that feel like? My heart beat strongly under the buttons of the navy dress, and my esophagus clenched. I stared up into the metal framework on the ceiling of the soundstage where lights hung like grapes on a vine. I breathed and let the feelings simmer and grow until the crew had set the lights. I sensed grips and gaffers respectfully walking around me, understanding that I was lying on the floor working. People who work on TV crews are the best. They are quiet and skilled and have a sixth sense about when to leave an actor alone because they are preparing to send a child off to war or do a love scene with a stranger. Makeup people came over to check my lipstick, and I let them, but I never lost the space I was in, that raw, almost magical space of allowing an imaginary circumstance to come to life.

The combination of my weight loss, my teaching (I had been teaching acting at Oberlin, and it sharpened my chops in all ways; teaching rocks), and my personal life (in that order) was all I needed to nail the scene. I lived through that moment, the moment of asking your partner to act, to be responsible, and to make a decision. I was saying, "Don't fuck with me," but really I was saying, "Don't fuck with my children," and everyone heard it as clear as a bell.

When we finished my coverage (when the camera is on me), the director and producer stood up from where they had been watching me on the monitor and applauded. They must have felt something, or they were recognizing that it's not easy to come back to a major TV show when you have been gone, then do what needed to be done in just a couple of takes. Chris squeezed my arm and gave me a wink, like, Nice job, sister. I have never felt so relieved or proud, and I had a feeling I was back. And, on TV anyway, I saved my marriage.

chapter 8

Now that I had work again as an actress, I figured I could justify hiring a part-time babysitter, right?

If you work even one day on an episode of a TV show, the shoot can take fifteen hours. You may have to leave home at any time from the dark of morning till the dark of night, and even though the second assistant director will try to give you ample notice of exactly when you will be working, sometimes you will be held on a "will notify," which means that they don't really have a clear idea of when they need you, so there is no way for you to time when you will have to jump into the van to New Jersey, miles and miles away from your children. Even though my parents were very generous about spotting me if I needed them to babysit, they had their own lives; I couldn't depend on them all the time and I didn't want to. My mother's mother, my grandmother Mimi, said, "Always have your own cigarettes," and I like to apply that kind of self-reliance to life as much as I can.

The customs of taking care of kids in Manhattan aren't

like those in other communities across the country, as far as I can tell. When I was living in Cambridge and in Oberlin, it was not unusual for a mother who lived down the lane to drop by with a kid or two and ask you to watch them while she went to the gym or the market. At first, I found this totally alien and questioned (to myself) why someone I sort of knew from the playground would be so loosey-goosey about leaving her little darlings with me just because I was over the age of eighteen and had a roof. But soon, this way of taking care of children just felt like part of life in the kind of community I admired and aspired to participate in. Easygoing, trusting, hey-no-problem kind of living. But I never fully got the hang of it, maybe because my children were too young, or because it was simply not my experience growing up in Manhattan. As I remember it, there was no real community in our building when I was a child. Everyone was friendly in the elevator, year after year, but I can't imagine my mother ever dropping us off in anyone's apartment (even our friends the Rosens, who lived on eleven) while she dashed to Associated, the grungy but menschy grocery store on Columbus Avenue. If anything, we went with her. So, while I don't remember other people's apartments in our building, I could describe every shelf and check-out person at Associated; it smelled like wet cardboard and cabbage. In the Big Apple, parents arrange formal playdates all the time, but to this day, this city is really a city, and I don't think a lot of moms just drop off their kids when they suddenly need to go to work. I'm not sure where half my kids' friends live! There aren't cul-de-sacs where the pack of bike-riding ten-year-olds all pile into one big kitchen and eat Fig Newtons under the watchful eye of a parent. We don't have swing sets in the backyard, where it's actually much more fun to have multiple four-year-olds playing than just one. New York is just different, harder. And I think it always has been.

So I needed to hire a babysitter. I thought there must be a college student somewhere in the five boroughs who needed a little extra money and who had schedule flexibility, in case I needed to be at work suddenly and for a long time. I put an ad on Craigslist. That possibly sounds a little wacko—wacko like Internet dating is wacko, because *it's on the Internet*—but I had just been teaching at a college, and those kids did practically everything on Craigslist or other sites like it. All these smart, funny, imaginative college kids used the World Wide Web with such frequency that I thought if I wanted to find a smart, funny, imaginative kid to help me out with the boys, I would join the revolution and log on.

And I found Erica. Erica came to the interview wearing a T-shirt with angel's wings on the back. Erica looked like a tall, Jewish, twenty-something Elizabeth Taylor. She wore Guatemalan crocheted beanie caps and spoke about something as banal as a dirty towel as if it were a unicorn. I think much of the world seemed magical to her, so she talked about everything as if it *were* magical—or maybe *she* was magical. Erica was also a *transition person*. She knew this about herself. One day while we were making turkey sandwiches in the kitchen, she said out of the blue, "I'm a transition person."

"Oh yeah?" I said, steadily spreading mayo across the 715-grain bread.

"I'm good at helping people move from one place to another.

That's why I'll be a good labor doula [something she was studying] and why I was good at working at the hospice. I'm good at helping people be born and die."

She spoke softly and very matter-of-factly, as if she were some kind of monk or clairvoyant, even though she was just from Philly.

"Oh," I said, sort of taken aback. It felt like when someone starts to talk about something icky, like dermatology. I want to be cool and join in, but it feels a little odd. "Well, that's a nice person to be."

"Yeah. Well, it's good I'm here, because you need me." She put down the wax-paper package the turkey was in, tilted her head, smiled, and said, "You and the boys are getting born again."

•   •   •

My children were never shy around Erica. They didn't even hide behind me the first time she walked in the door. Usually when someone new appeared, the boys went behind me or under a bed. Wallace was worse off than James in the hiding department. James was little and, thankfully, still in the clouds that God provides to protect babies from tuning in to life's harsher sides. Wallace was four, and I guess the deal with being four is that those clouds begin to part, and you start to see what's really going on.

Erica entered our apartment, picked up James, and opened her mouth wide—making no noise at all—and the two of them cracked up. Seeing this, Wallace bashfully asked if she would like to see his drum set, which my father and I had assembled in the living room with the help of a tattooed drum tech named Ralph. Wallace then took her hand to guide her into the living room. My mother and I stood astonished on the sidelines.

"Wow," she said.

*   *   *

It was a relief to have some outside child care in the apartment, even if it was only for ten hours a week. Taking care of small children by yourself is bloody hard, and I don't think either my mother or I would ever say that parenting the two-to-six-year-old set is our strongest suit anyway. We aren't the worst. My mother has countless times charmed a toddler by allowing him or her to play with her powder compact. And I remember sitting on the cobalt-blue, linoleum kitchen floor with her when she, in a rather uncharacteristic Lucille Ball moment, dumped with abandon all the Easter egg dyes into one spaghetti pot because I asked what would happen if we did. Brown Easter eggs is what happens. She also lovingly empathized with my inconsolable tears the day I grew out of my red leather party shoes at age three. (Those shoes didn't come in a larger size; older girls wore black patent leather.) I remember the look of determination on her face as she swept her hair behind her ear and, tugging in vain, tried to wedge the red slipper on over the white sock that was turned down at my ankle.

I *hope* good mother moments like these are nestled in my kids' brains; I hope snow picnics and line-up back-scratching and tossing their overly salted (my fault) shrimp dinner into the ocean to see how many crabs would come (a million) are in there. But I know there will be a lot of not-so-pleasant memories, too, like the not-so-pleasant childhood memories I have of my mother. My mother, like me, sometimes didn't get it right. We are organized, we make routines, we maintain bedtimes and set tables, but we have anxieties about mothering the young child. No preschool teachers on that side of the family, no one of that sort for generations.

The same unease is not the case when it comes to animals. My mother can tell within five seconds if a dog on the street is lost or not. She can look a gargantuan bull in the eye (in a barn), make a bull sound with her mouth and nose, and scratch the curly part in between the beast's eyes as if she were Artemis. One of the reasons I know how to love at all is because I watched how much my mother loved our dog Angus—but kids aren't dogs.

This parenting trouble ebbs—it isn't there for the entire time. My mother is brilliant at teenagers (and when I watch her walk to her garden hand in hand with a child to go check on the size of a zucchini, I'm thinking she has an affinity for grandparenting that her mother didn't have). And I, maybe unlike my mother, who went back to work when I was three weeks old, was undaunted by infants. I loved them. I loved watching their tiny bodies jolt out in a Moro reflex if they were startled by the wind knocking around a door. I loved nursing and taking a bath with a creature that felt more like a tree frog gripping onto my breast than a human. I even loved when they screamed their heads off. It's like their wailing went right through me as I stared in wonder into their giant, wide open, tiny mouths.

But sometimes those toddler years felt (sorry, God) grueling.

• • •

I remember reading somewhere that you must talk to your baby constantly: changing them, pushing the stroller, et cetera. It makes them smarter. So from the moment Wallace was born, I talked and talked and *talked* to him at all times.

"Wallace, I am walking down Massachusetts Avenue, where we reside in Cambridge, Massachusetts, and you are in your baby carriage, or pram. (I, following my mother's lead, pepper my language with bits of British, French, and Spanish to mix it up. Unlike my mother, I'm not fluent in any language other than English.) Your father teaches the English language here, specializing in poetry at Harvard University. It is a beautiful, crisp, autumnal day. I can feel the northwest wind gusting mightily off the Charles River. Without this woven, wool sweater, I would be frigid." I would overly describe everything that was happening to my eighteen-month-old, and when I had nothing left to say, I would just recite a string of interesting words. Aubergine. Crocodile. Sopressata. Wilderness. Triathlon.

I wish I loved those monologues as I loved the Moro reflexes, but really, all that talking felt forced and lonely.

There are parents who can't get enough of taking the eighteen-month-old to the playground or who think it's hilarious when their little children splash water all over the bathroom, but for me taking care of little ones was a challenge. And then something terrible happened that not only made our lives feel fraught and vulnerable, but made me think that the universe was taking the very thing that had specifically flummoxed so many of the women I came from, and was forcing me to face it and figure it out, head on and alone. *I* was a single mother of toddlers; it was almost like a joke.

Now that my children are bigger, and our time together seems to be going too fast, I understand what people were saying when they urged me to "enjoy it, because soon they will be grown and gone." I remember my sister-in-law Shari, in her straightforward, unashamed, and Midwestern way, telling me, as I picked up the bowl of peas for the seventh time, to *love it*. And she was right, because *now* my heart contorts when I think about them staying later and later at school. It takes my breath away when one of them wakes up in the morning, has a pee, and heads for the kitchen without needing to crawl into my bed, or runs down a dock with his friends and doesn't look back. As I see their little bodies strengthen and grow lean, I know that in what seems like a second, they won't pour their water right to the brim of their cup or fall asleep at seven forty-five in the evening, and they won't out of habit reach their little hands toward mine at the crosswalk or run toward me as fast as they can across the big yard of their school when I come to pick them up at twenty minutes past three. They will still need to be looked after, but more by girlfriends and wives than by their mum. They will grow and be gone, just like everyone said. (Oh, if you knew how I am weeping right now, as I type this.)

But when my husband left me they were toddlers, and because of a little work, I got to have the winged Erica help me. Erica, who understood that transitions, whether you are going through them at age fifteen months or at age seventy-three, are smoother if there is someone alongside you saying, "Don't worry, I'm here too."

chapter 9

O ne evening I was standing over the stove, sautéing lemon
sole for the boys, when the phone on the wall rang.

"Hi, Isabel? It's Andrew Archie," said a very matter-of-
fact, rather nasally voice.

"Oh, hi, Mr. Archie," I said, and then we had a few ex-
changes of polite conversation before I offered to get my mother.
Andrew Archie is the priest from the church that we go to in
the summer in Maine. I'm not especially religious, but I have
to say that if I do have a religion in me, it's because of that
church. It sits nestled into the repose of a steep hill in a small
forest. From almost any pew, if you look out a window you can
see shimmering birch leaves, and if you take a deep breath
(which happens almost instantaneously when you see how
green those leaves are) you smell one-hundred-year-old woods
and the sea. My mother was the warden of the church at the
time Andrew Archie made this phone call, so I assumed he
was calling to talk with her.

"Oh, no," he said, "I am calling to talk to you."

Oh my God, I thought. *Is this* priest *really calling to offer me some advice because my life is in ruins? Sweet Lord, let that not be true. Please, no, please.*

"I am going to be in New York soon and I want to come see you."

"Oh, yeah, I know," I stammered. "But you know, I'm really fine and totally swamped. I'm trying to start Wallace off in school and James is so little and I don't have a sitter very much and it's just—"

"Yes, I understand, but I would like to see you," he said kindly but firmly.

"Umm." I fiddled with a tree of broccoli and watched James break uncooked noodles in half on the kitchen floor.

"Okay, umm, I can't really go out to lunch, or maybe I could, but I'd have to ask my parents to babysit, and they are really busy, too. And James is tricky to get to sleep." (A lie. The child falls asleep like a Labrador puppy, even before his head hits the pillow.)

Will anything *get me out of this?*

"I can come to you."

"Well, James goes to sleep at around one. If you don't mind Wallace making a *lot* of noise, you could come over for lunch."

"That sounds fine. I'll have whatever you are feeding the boys."

I tried to get out of this lunch at least three more times, but he was having none of it. I'm not even sure that the conference he said he was going to wasn't made up, because he seemed to have so much flexibility. Why was I resisting? Wasn't it what people did in these circumstances? Seek out a priest for guidance? What was I so frightened I would say? I felt I had done something against God. I had not been able to save my marriage or I had not fought hard enough to keep Josiah from falling in love with that other girl. I had failed, divorce is a failure, and even though I knew Andrew Archie wasn't coming over to tell me that, I felt ashamed and in need of privacy. I also didn't want him to tell me Josiah was going to go to hell or something. I felt very defensive and protective of him still. Plus, the boys and I really did look pathetic—brave, but pathetic.

Thursday arrived. I procrastinated and didn't organize lunch. My mother offered to help by cooking. She and my father were going to be out, but she had offered to make a soup and sandwiches. (And it would have been a humdinger of a soup, too. Probably a potato leek, or a "Senlis soup," after the place in France where she learned to cook it.) I declined. For some reason I felt obligated to feed the man who was coming to offer help. Only half an hour before he was to arrive, I ended up hauling both boys in the stroller two avenues over to Barney Greengrass, a famous, hundred-year-old Jewish deli. It didn't even occur to me at the time how humorous it was that I got classic Jewish food to break bread with the Episcopalian rector, but Mr. Archie may have noticed it, because when I brought him into the kitchen to plate up the matzo ball soup, whitefish salad, and latkes, I noticed a little smile cross his face.

I put James down for a nap and Wallace in front of the video of Paul Simon's concert, *Graceland*, while Mr. Archie waited for me in the living room, seated in my mother's chair.

He balanced his plate and bowl on his lap (matzo ball soup is sloshy) and navigated sour cream adeptly while I told my story. I could never tell the story of what happened without some emotion rearing up. It felt like a confession every time, but now I was in front of an actual man of the cloth. I tried very hard not to cry. You will not break me, Priest. I defiantly gave my thin plan for the future and I asked him not to be mad at Josiah (whom he knew from summers in Maine) because I couldn't bear it. I felt defensive, but soft. I could hardly look at him, and didn't eat a thing. I could tell that he wanted to coat me in sympathy and warmth, but he also was picking up that if he was too nice to me I would break down and not be able to recover. Sometimes the hardest thing to handle is kindness.

It was only two in the afternoon. Wallace started calling from the other room (Ladysmith Black Mambazo will hold a four-year-old's attention for only so long), and it was clear that it was time for Mr. Archie to go. Although I don't remember them, he did say helpful things to me during that meal, and of course just seeing him proved to be more soothing than I ever would have guessed, but as he was leaving, he said something that I will never forget.

"I just want you to know one thing, Isabel." He looked at me so sincerely through his wire-rimmed glasses and with so much love. "God has a wallet in his back pocket and in it is a picture of you."

He wanted to tell me that God loved me. Did I feel loved

by God? I still don't know the answer to that question. I believe in God, because this life is way too amazing to not believe in God. To me, all you have to do is look at a lion or at moss to believe in God. But did I believe that God loved me? Mr. Archie believed that my troubles would feel lighter if I did.

chapter 10

In 1977 there was a massive, and now very famous, blackout
in New York City. My brother Andrew and I shared the room
that I would eventually, twenty-plus years later, move back
into, and at the moment the blackout began we were fast asleep,
aided by the hallway light that my parents always left on
for us.

That night, I remember the feeling of the darkness becoming suddenly even darker, and the surprise of that woke me up.
Moments later, my parents both came rushing in. It was well
into the evening, and they must have had a couple of glasses
of wine with dinner; they were excited.

"Kids! Kids!" My mother went to my brother's bed and my
father went to mine.

"Wake up! You have to see this!" My father's face was joyful. They pulled us out of our beds, guiding us through the
dark by our shoulders, and rushed us up to the huge living
room window. My brother and I, freaked out but thrilled to be
awake, scrambled onto the built-in window seat and looked

out over the dark park on our hands and knees. Although only on the seventh floor, Apartment 7A was blessed with an unencumbered, treetop view of Central Park.

"Just watch," my father whispered.

Starting out to the left, uptown, big chunks of the buildings on Fifth Avenue began to go black. Boom. Boom. Boom. All the way down into the Fifties, where you couldn't see anymore. And then we were all in the glorious dark, together.

In the 1970s, when we were little, nobody thought much about child-safe window bars, but mere days after Wallace, James, and I arrived in New York from Ohio, the safety bars had to be installed, as the law now requires—bars across the big, beautiful windows in Apartment 7A. The building's super and his assistant arrived at my parents' door holding armfuls of black iron poles and drills that looked like semiautomatic weapons. My mother's face fell.

"Hello, gentlemen! Those are all going up, huh?" my father said evenly.

"Yes," said Aldo in his thick Russian accent. "It's the law."

He and his crony then proceeded to drill the long strips of black metal into the walls, blocking the charming window with ominous jail bars so my children wouldn't fall out. We stood behind the men and watched. The incarceration metaphor was so obvious that none of us made a joke about Rikers Island (the maximum-security prison for New York City), but I wished someone had. My mother went into her room, the only place where she could get away. Dad bravely said it was a bummer, but we would get used to it.

"It's not Iraq," he declared, because the war in Iraq was in full swing then.

It wasn't Iraq, but it was a bummer. A big bummer.

So, first we imprisoned my parents, messing with what had been their magical view of Central Park. And then we brought another scourge of small children upon them. Sickness. Terrible sickness. Flu.

• • •

Sickness and heartbreak, they go together beautifully. But the stiff-upper-lip, pull-up-your-socks attitude that my parents and I had been embracing got pummeled by the flu. This was a flu like none I had seen or have seen since. It was medieval. And it was gothic. And I felt like Marianne Dashwood in Jane Austen's *Sense and Sensibility*. Heartbroken by the dashing, but weak-of-character, John Willoughby, the unmarried Marianne comes down with a dreadful flu (because she was on a forlorn, heartsick walk on the moors in the driving rain) that almost kills her. Her devoted elder sister, Elinor, sits by her sickbed, cooling her pale white brow with rags soaked in alcohol and water until she revives. I didn't have an elegant, elder, spinster sister who had nothing to do but worry about me. I had comatose parents in their bed down the hall. They had also caught the nasty bug (but caught it even worse than the boys or I had, because they are older). I also had two stir-crazy, snotty toddlers who had been so sick that green mucus had come out of the corners of their eyes and who were now getting over their flu and ready to go outside, even though it was frigid, gray, wet, and horrible in the park. I remember glimpsing my father through the crack in the door; he was lying, mouth open and very white, in his bed. He hadn't been out of pajamas in days. I thought, *I am going to kill them. My children and their germs are going to kill my parents, and everyone will think I did it on purpose so that I could have their rent-controlled apartment.* I would haul my delirious body, heavy with disease, toward the kitchen to make the boys' breakfast. I was so exhausted I would pause in front of the television, where the boys had been stuck for the last three hours, and blindly watch a nature show until I saw some *good* mother turtle feed her young, then I'd realize my own young were starving. In my haze I thought, *My God, I'm going to kill my parents with germs and starve my children to death because I can't physically make it to the kitchen.* If everybody got killed off by this epic flu but me, it would be like I was eighteen again, starting off in the world free of responsibility, no baggage, no worries. Thankfully, nobody met their demise, but it did make all the responsibility, baggage, and worry a lot more acute.

The days went by like chilled honey. Winter days are not short, they are just dark, and these felt eternal. I could feel every second of every minute. At night, through the bars on the windows, you could see the lights of Fifth Avenue across the park, promising other apartments, filled with happy people and happy lives. They seemed as far away as the stars. You know the image of all the Darling children in *Peter Pan* looking out their window into the dark night, seeking Neverland? I felt like the opposite. I felt like I was in Neverland, looking in all the windows at the families, wishing and hoping that one day I would be inside one of my own.

At night the boys' father would call.

"Hello." My swollen throat barely let out a whisper; and if I saw it was a call from Ohio, I maybe made it a little worse.

"Oh, hi, you sound awful," he said in his totally healthy-no-kids-around voice.

"We are sick. We are so fucking siiiiccckkkk."

"Wow, yeah, it sounds like it. I'm sorry."

"Yeah, well."

"Are the boys around?" Interested in them. Not me. There were moments when I thought sheer guilt would make him come back to me. But it didn't. I'm sure he felt guilty, but the bigger point was that even if he did, that wasn't going to make him fall out of love with someone else, or restart something with me. He had moved on, and I was going to have to, too, sick or not. I would race around following the kids with the phone in my hand, trying to make them have a meaningful conversation.

Eventually, illness lifted enough from our house for me to take Wallace to school. He only went until 12:30, so when I got back from picking him up, Erica would be waiting with James, who was about to go down for a nap. (She got to our apartment at 8:30 and left at 1:00 p.m. She would pass the torch to me, and I was on duty with the boys for the rest of the day.) It was always a bummer when Erica left, not so much because I was on duty, but because it made me feel lonely. Erica was fun. On walks in the park with James, she would collect small branches so that later she and the boys could make dream catchers: She and Wallace and James would sit at the little blue table, threading brightly colored beads through kitchen string, winding that beaded thread around the knobs on the branches like a spider's web. She hung the small handmade nets above the boys' crib and bed and assured them that their bad dreams would be caught by the web, and the good dreams would tumble through and fall straight into their heads while they were sleeping. Every day that she watched James, she had a plan for him, some mission to accomplish or adventure to seek out. The moment she walked in the door in the morning, she declared it a letter-of-the-alphabet day, like on *Sesame Street*.

On this particular day (maybe it was the letter "R" day—red, ride, roof, rope), I said good-bye to Erica and went with Wallace to sit with my mother, who was eating a bowl of plain spaghetti on her chair in the living room. The living room had seen better days. The wear and tear of little ones playing in it all day was starting to show. The sofas that Arlo the cat had massacred with his claws were just about to be re-covered when, after our arrival, it was thought better to wait. Why spend all that money when suddenly all of our lives were in flux? None of us knew what was coming next, and our current predicament far from called for new chintz.

My mother did not look up at me when I came into the living room. She was seated in her chair that faced away from the window. My father's chair was opposite hers. The lunch she was eating on her lap was naked pasta—no tomato sauce, no Parmesan. I don't think it even had butter on it. Clearly, something was off, way off. Even when my mother is alone for dinner, she cooks. She'll get herself a beautiful liver (knowing nobody else in our family likes innards) and prepare it carefully; if herbs are called for, they will be there, and she'll pour herself a big glass of red wine just to enjoy it all the more. She might heat up a Stouffer's Turkey Tetrazzini, but it will have a tomato salad with it, and maybe some fresh chopped parsley for color. The point is, she cares about her food. Seeing her lunch on flavorless pasta in the middle of the day was like walking in on somebody else drinking scotch in the morning. *"Whoooosh! BANG!"* There came metal crashing sounds. *"BANG!"* Wallace had begun to play with Matchbox cars that had belonged to my brother.

"Wallace, please try to do that quietly. Granny is eating." My mother kept twirling the white-ish noodles around and around, not looking up and not saying it was okay if Wallace wanted to play in there. I felt like taking Wallace and leaving, but I didn't have anywhere to go, Erica had gone, and James was sleeping. I didn't think it would be a good time to ask my mother to watch over James.

Mum, did I ruin your life?

That's what I wanted to say, because I felt like I had. Maybe not just because of the divorce; maybe also because my hair had always been knotted as a child, or because I hadn't learned to read easily, or because I was overly self-involved, or because of just a gut feeling, a fear she had that I would end up on the losing end of things in life, that I was a misfit. I felt like maybe she didn't even like me because of some of those things. And maybe she wished I was someone else so she didn't have to have that poisonous feeling of disliking her own child, even if it was just a little bit. I know that she feels close to me and *I do know that she loves me*, but if she had those complicated feelings about me, she must have hated them, and tried to shelter me from them. This was a feeling I sometimes had, but if I'm right, it must have made her sick in the middle of the night that she felt that way. And that was before I brought so much complication to live with her—divorce, small boys, and bars across her windows.

I really didn't have to ask if I'd ruined her life, because her silence and angry twirling were telling me very clearly: Yes. Yes, I had. I got the message loud and clear, and I got angry. I was thinking, *I am trying the best I can, you bitch. I have always tried so hard. What can I do to make you like me?* Wallace got louder and louder. My mother looked like she was going to explode, but her face wasn't red and inflamed, it was steely cold.

It was a look that said, *Get the fuck out of my house and take your loud, abandoned children with you! Make your lowlife ex-husband take you back! Give me back my office!*

I feared she was dying to yell.

But there was a four-year-old in the room, and we couldn't, either of us, yell.

No matter how much we both wanted to.

Eventually, my distraught mother pointedly and clamorously dropped her fork in the middle of the unfinished plate, got up, and left the room, without saying a word.

I looked out at the park, a view that had so often changed a feeling in me, given me something to aim for, be inspired by, take comfort in, but I couldn't find any answers in all the wintry mist. I felt so bad for messing up and for troubling my parents, and Wallace, who was now tired of the cars, was looking more lost than ever, lying on the floor, also staring out into nothing.

It felt like nobody wanted us, and we needed everybody.

chapter 11

I bet most people like school vacations, but during that first post-marriage year, I found school vacations daunting. (I still do, sort of, except I don't have to make lunch at 7:00 a.m. every day during school vacations, and that's pretty nice.) First of all, without school, your children briefly lose an important little community that might (depending on what's happening at home) be the sturdier part of their life. Secondly, in order to deal with the chaos of children, parents must carefully develop well-structured routines, little organizing systems to guide the family smoothly through the week. Vacations screw those all up. And if you live in New York, the midwinter break is also challenging because it's cold.

Josiah's parents lived in Florida and felt terrible about everything that Josiah and I were going through. They were *his* parents after all, but we had been close and had spent lots of time together during our marriage. When the dreaded winter break came in late February, they kindly invited the boys and me down to their house. They paid for it, too, as that was the only way I was flying anywhere those days. I felt odd going down to a house and family that I once belonged to and now didn't, but I wanted my boys to feel love from anywhere it could possibly come from, and some of it was coming from Florida, so that's where we went.

Josiah and I decided to split the vacation. I would go down for the first half and he would meet me there and take over for the second. I had a small hope, tiny really, that maybe on the night that we overlapped we would reconcile. Maybe the sunshine and palm trees would melt us back together. I gave this hope about a 1 percent chance, but it caused me to go to Banana Republic with Bess anyway to buy a new T-shirt or two.

"I don't know how they will be able to look you in the face," Bess said while checking out the heel of a shoe.

"I know," I agreed sheepishly and picked up a sandal. "But I think we all just feel crummy about it and would rather get along and keep our focus on the children. I'm sure we'll just talk about the weather and endlessly plan meals." I said this, emphasizing my point with the sandal, then I put the shoe down again without ever really looking at it.

"Okay, but I think you should look great the whole time. Try on *this*. You glow in pink." She held up a diaphanous blouse.

"It's going to be so weird. I used to think of their house as mine, sort of. At least, enough to go into the kitchen in the middle of the night in my nightgown. Now it's like I'm a stranger, with their grandkids." I put the blouse back on the rack.

"What you really need to go down to Florida is a big diamond ring. I hate that you don't get to wear your engagement ring anymore and *look at these!*"

She grabbed my hand and pulled me around to the faux jewelry case. There were four or five six-to-ten carat "diamond" rings.

"Wow," I said.

"They are so good. I bet no one will ever know if it's real or not. They might just think that you have met an Argentinean polo player who has madly fallen in love with you and the boys and has given you a great big honking ring."

I looked at her cockeyed.

"What? You look like a *supermodel!*"

Bess is always saying I look like a supermodel to boost my self-confidence. It's not true, but if your best friend wants to say you look like Gisele, what the hell.

"I'll give it to you," she said and marched off to get the saleswoman.

• • •

At the time, Josiah's mother and stepfather's house in Florida was in a gated community with a golf course and a big man-made lake. You got the feeling it was all built ten minutes ago and for nine of the ten minutes the maintenance guys had been spraying pesticides and mowing the grass; it was so manicured. But it was warm there and pretty, with hibiscus everywhere and many different-shaped palm trees. The boys thought they were in paradise. There were huge, veiny banyan trees that they would climb all over, and contrary to everything else there, you got the feeling those trees grew a thousand years ago. Whenever I saw Wallace and James in those trees, I thought we were in paradise, too. My ex-mother-in-law, Julia, has beautiful sheets. (Oh, how I loathe the prefix "ex." I hate all the divorce terminology: "ex," "step," "half." All of it is distancing, at arm's length, one step away from something *real*. For people who need togetherness and unity after a traumatizing rupture such as divorce, language doesn't give you much of a break.) Julia takes care of everything meticulously, so her things last for decades. Every sheet set has careful embroidery, a scalloped edge, and winding, pale ivy or fluttery wisteria. Nothing bright, just elegant and ironed. Those sheets made me feel like I was in paradise, too.

If I imagined what it would be like to alight on your almost-ex in-laws in the middle of a troubling marital breakup that heavily involved their son and his mistress, I would have imagined there would be a lot of hashing it out. Maybe that comes from the movies, because, really, the only people who will talk ad infinitum about your divorce with you are your girlfriends. Most other people, like parents, tend to avoid the topic in an attempt to make things seem normal. And actually, my ex-parents-in-law were so busy trying to give us a good time, they didn't even return the ironic, pained looks I would give them or seem to catch on at all to how totally weird it all was. But if I thought they were missing something, they were not. If I thought they didn't have anything to say, I was wrong. They had as much to say as I did; they just were not going to ruin the children's time with a bad conversation about something they had very little control over. But I was determined to have a conversation. I wanted answers from them because they had raised him.

One night after the boys were in bed, Julia came to my

room to say good night. I was sitting on the bed, leaning against the headboard, with my knees up.

Josiah was coming the next day, and I would be leaving the following. I don't remember the first part of the conversation, because it must have been about travel plans or laundry (Julia will wash a chocolate-stained shirt until it almost has the price tag on it again) and how we would work it all out. As much as I can appreciate the small-talk side of things, the making-things-nice-for-the-children tactic, I couldn't stand it anymore, and I said something about not being sure I could handle what the future held, and marveled at what on earth Josiah thought he was doing.

"Josiah believes, Isabel, that you are very strong and will be able to handle it, to get through this hard part and come out the other side."

She looked so perfect. She is the most beautiful woman. She has thick, white hair that practically nobody has. Most of my childhood (I have known her since I was around seven or eight) she wore it up in a chignon. I remember looking at the back of her head in church in Maine and thinking to myself when I should have been listening to the sermon, *Goodness, Mrs. Byers has beautiful hair.* My mother told me she did that, too. As Julia grew older, she cut it shorter, and even though I know she didn't go to a hairdresser every day, it always looked as if she had. She wore pale silk scarves around her neck tucked into a blouse. She is ladylike and elegant. Nobody would say otherwise.

Anyway, she stood in front of me, and instead of letting what she had said about her son believing in my strength pass, instead of making it easy for her to leave me alone in the beautiful bed she had made for me, I decided to give it to her.

"Oh, did he say that? Really. Do you get how *convenient* that is for him?" I raised my voice, which made her tense just a little bit. She knew I could lose my temper if I wanted to, and I bet she really didn't want me to.

"That is such bullshit, Julia! *Your son* has left me totally high and dry! What am I going to do? How am I going to take care of *our children?* He's just off with Sylvia, and I don't think he gives a good Goddamn what happens to us, because obviously he thinks I'm strong enough to handle it. Well, what if I'm not?" I said, and started crying, although I was enraged.

"I know you can, Isabel," she said, not losing her cool, standing her ground, staring at me coiled on the bed, like a snake (with a big, fake diamond ring on) whipping around for the kill.

"You don't know how this feels!" I spat in a self-righteous tone. "Your son did something *wrong* and you should feel ashamed of him."

Not losing composure or her loyalty, she said, "I am very sorry for how Josiah has handled this, Isabel, but he *is* a good person."

"He is *not* a good person. Good people don't do this! You don't know, you don't know what I am going through! *You don't know!*"

I was pointing at her and crying, bracing my back against the upholstered headboard and driving my feet into the sheets, pushing them away from me until they bunched at the bottom of the bed. I was already ashamed of my outburst, but my eyes never left her.

For one moment, my seventy-something-year-old former mother-in-law in her well-assembled, pale-peach-and-cream linen outfit and her perfect hair and her soft, sophisticated southern accent, cracked.

When she had been my age, her husband, Josiah's father, had left her, and she'd had to take care of two impossibly tiny boys, too, and for one moment that frightened, young, and undone woman came out and pointed right back at me.

"Yes, I do know. Yes. I. Do. Know," she said to me, as if she was only going to say it to me once in her entire life and she wanted me to hear it.

She was breathless and my breath was taken away. My entire marriage, my whole life, really, I had seen her as supple, composed, unflappable; she is like a rose. At that moment, I understood that her composure was something she had built, something she had constructed, something she had needed to get through what had been taken away from her. We were the same. She did know what I was feeling, and once she rapidly regained her composure, she told me from the bottom of her heart and with all she had learned, her best instruction: "You move on, Isabel. You do the best you can and you move on."

That shut me up. Who did I think I was to put someone, who was only trying to help, in her place—and *his mother* at that? I can't think of one time when my ex-mother-in-law wasn't kindly, trying her best to either do something nice for me or for my children. In retrospect, it must have been a total drag to have me down to Florida. I'm sure even though we *did* talk about menus and where more sunscreen was, I never let them off the hook for what their son had done, and she just took it. The indignation that I felt all the time narrowed my view. I might have neglected to suppose that she knew another side. It could likely have been that Josiah revealed feelings to her that he never shared with me. Her son was more important to her than I was, by a long shot. Nothing could get in the way of her fierce and unflagging love for him.

I had to remember that there were people other than me who were affected by this divorce, that I wasn't the only one hurting, and that everyone hurts in different ways. It was generous of her to advise me to hold on and keep living, but if I was smart, I wouldn't turn my back on what she told me Josiah had said: that I was strong.

part
III

chapter 12

I guess it did come off like I *needed* to find a husband. I had very little money, two boys who needed a father figure, and I was young, sort of. I would love, *love* to sit here and write that I gained inner strength, got all the love I needed from my children, friends, and family, and found peace in the idea that I might never be married again. How I wanted that to be true. How I didn't want to feel desperate and in need of a man. And it is true that I worked it out so I didn't *need* to remarry. Because of my parents' inexpensive, rent-controlled apartment (not only could I live in it for the rest of my days but my children could live in it for the rest of theirs), a job on television (and if that ended, I did have arms, legs, and a college degree), and the fact that public schools existed, I would be fine. Very many people work it out with far fewer resources; my children and I were going to survive. The father figure part, though, had nothing to do with money, and I did feel that my boys needed one of those sometime soon. Freud said, "I cannot think of any need in childhood as strong as the need for a father's protection." I don't know if it's the strongest need, but from where I was standing, it struck me as pretty obvious that *the father* was very important to my boys. They did actually have a father, even though, at the time, he felt far away. And they did have my father, which gave me peace of mind, but my father was in his seventies. My instinct was that if I did fall in love with a nice man, it wouldn't be a bad thing for all of us.

Was I in need or in want? I wanted my little nuclear family that I'd had in Ohio. If I couldn't have my husband and our life together back, I wanted a new family. I wanted a husband to love, to cook for, to laugh about something a kid said, to solve in-law problems with, to help me gather receipts for taxes, find lost keys for, borrow sweaters from, fill out school applications with—to share my life. There seems to be shame in saying that you want love. There is greater shame in saying that you need it. Maybe it's because I went to all-girls schools in the Northeast or experienced my formative years on the heels of the women's movement in New York City, but the notion or pressure that one should be able to "do it" (whatever "it" might be—work, social life, sex life, even raising children) by yourself was always hovering and making me, at least, feel kind of guilty for wanting Sir Lancelot *to marry me*. (Ironic that I was always being told to read Edith Wharton and Jane Austen, even Dickens, all of them chock-o-block with love and family and marriage.)

I don't think the social pressure to be self-sustaining is only a women's issue, or a heterosexual issue, or any one group's issue; it's seen as unattractive to need or want any kind of relationship (there are entire books written on how to pretend you don't want and need). But we are humans and we do both. I think if society hadn't intervened, we would all still sleep in piles like gorillas.

My first cousin from my mother's side of the family, who looks exactly like me but is six inches shorter, is a Buddhist, and calm, smart, and steady, and around this time she recommended a book called something like *When the Shit Hits the Fan*, or *When Your Life Is Over*—something fitting like that. As soon as I could, I hauled the two boys to the bookstore on Broadway to get it. It might have even been in the Zen section, with all the books written by famous monks. Later, as soon as the kids were asleep, I sank into bed with this book. I was hoping that it would be filled with chilled-out hope and messages of don't-worry-it-will-all-turn-out-all-right (which is the only thing anyone really wants to hear in the kind of circumstances I was in), but this was not that book. This book was about a woman who gets left by her husband (right, same as me), finds deep peace with that situation (good, like that notion), and then . . . *becomes a nun.*

Okay, I wish that could have been something to consider, but really, becoming a nun was not in the cards. I don't have what it takes to be so selfless, open-hearted, and smart. (I've only met a few nuns, but they all seemed awfully smart.) And although I tried to, I was not able to come up with any big beef against men, either. I guess I love men, or am too ruled by schoolgirl, unrealistic notions of romance with them. Maybe all those John Hughes movies I saw in the eighties took hold of me in a way that I will never be released from, but I will always strive for the happy ending where I get kissed by Eric Stoltz. And you know what? Those movies were successful because other people feel the same as I do.

The thought of another husband, not the reality of it but the thought of it, was a comfort. Even though I felt low-grade panic that I wouldn't find love again, I reasoned that there are many men in the world; I had a chance of finding someone to share my life with; math was on my side. And, to repeat myself, I personally don't think there is anything wrong with striving to find happiness with another human being; isn't that life's entire point?

So, on the one hand, my belief in romance kept my hopes alive; on the other hand, though, there was Lily Bart. Lily Bart is the heroine of Edith Wharton's novel *The House of Mirth*. I had read the book about a year before I came back to New York with my boys. It's a great book, and it's devastating. It's about a twenty-nine-year-old woman from the upper classes in late nineteenth-century New York who screws up about whom to marry and ends up not marrying anyone; she dies alone and poor and knowing that she screwed up. She is offered proposals from men she loves and from men she doesn't love but who have a lot of money. She makes all kinds of clumsy, bad decisions (she doesn't have parents guiding her, which is unfortunate; instead, she has a guardian with ulterior motives). In the end, she overdoses (unclear if on purpose) on sleeping medicine.

When you are happily married and the mother of a solid little family living in Ohio, and you read *The House of Mirth*, you see Lily's tragic poor decision-making at a distance. You shake your head, sigh, and feel the slightest bit smug that you are not her. But that whole feeling changes when you are a single mother living with your parents. Suddenly you see that book in a brand-new, not-so-amusing light. The world could either be your oyster, or if you screw up, it could be the place where you die sadly of an Ambien overdose because you made poor choices.

What if I screwed it up like Lily Bart? What if I didn't learn from my mistakes? I still believed I had to marry for love, but what if I fell in love with someone who wasn't appropriate? Never mind money, what if the person was nice at first and seemed good enough, but then was mean to my kids? What if there was no more love out there to be had? What if there were no more good men in the world? What about Cinderella? Her father's second marriage was a disaster. What if I was too selective and missed the boat entirely? Lily Bart is fictitious, but you just know there are a ton of real Lily Barts out in the world, certainly in New York. I had to make the right decisions. It felt like even what side of the street I chose to walk down might have repercussions. I walked around the Upper West Side a lot with the boys, because we didn't have much else to do. And as we would approach a corner I'd say, "Boys, should we go down Eighty-fifth Street or Eighty-fourth?" Then one of them would call out a street, and down we would go. I told myself I was teaching them about their new surroundings and about numbers, but really, I was giving them some of my burden. The very heavy burden of getting it right.

. . .

I had to get us out of our cocoon and socialize. Luckily, I was living in my hometown, where many of my childhood friends had settled:

"Why don't we have a weekly pizza date where you come over with the boys?"

"We can meet you anywhere—the museum? Pizza?"

"We would *love* to have you over to hang with us; we can do something easy like order a pizza."

"Come over any afternoon. We're here. We can talk and (the kids) can eat a pizza."

Thank God for pizza, the universal food of inexpensive, round goodness and ease that basically can sustain everybody. Many a late afternoon, I felt that old friends, especially other mothers, were lifting great wings for me and the boys to duck under—and there would be pizza.

Getting divorced made me feel like the first girl in my class to get braces. I was doing something that others would unfortunately have to experience, but this experience was still uncharted territory for most. Suddenly, I spoke a different language. I spoke divorce. I could riff on lawyers and custody and sleeping alone in a way that most of my friends could not, thankfully. But it was stranger-in-a-strange-land time. I felt left out of what is supposed to happen. I was on the outside of the heavily participated-in norm. I was a "single mother." Different. Other.

When I took the kids over to visit with a mother whose husband was at work, that felt fine. Yes, the discussions could head in a weightier direction, but more often than not, those conversations were thoughtful and clarifying. Hillary Clinton wasn't kidding when she famously said it takes a village to raise a child; we were women and children hanging out together, and that scenario is ages old. What felt odd was attending a weekend playdate with other families. I would heave the stroller into some apartment with my two little guys, a bit frazzled, kind of harried; smile, and give the "I'm fine!" face; then proceed to get everything organized—all boots and scarves and snowsuits off, and all polite hellos delivered—by myself, with no help from a husband, which made everyone else at the playdate anxious, I think.

Here is what the mom/dad or mom/mom or dad/dad conversation sounds like at one of these gatherings.

"Hon, will you just, yeah, that one, no, his yellow thing . . . Thanks," says one parent.

"What, bunny? You want to go potty? Okay. Um, Hon, I'm taking—Yeah, okay, you stay here with him. What? No, I have the wipes. Don't worry. Watch him, will you? He almost spilled that! Now. Okay, sweetie, let's go," says the other.

Then one goes with one kid to the potty while the other stays with the leftover kid, making sure he doesn't hit anyone or fall out the window.

Even though my friends were not practiced in having a single parent in the mix, overall they instinctively seemed to know what to do.

At a birthday party for my godson, a father pretended for a moment to be a gorilla. He got on all fours, curled his fingers under, tilted his back upward, and started oofing and grunting.

Surprisingly, exactly like a gorilla. Wallace, who had been sitting like a lonely guy in the corner of the L-shaped sectional, sucking his thumb, looked out of the side of his eye, and without removing thumb from mouth, started to giggle at the daddy gorilla. The dad took note and, although I'm sure he hadn't planned on doing the gorilla thing for long, played as the gorilla with Wallace for the rest of the party. Wallace turned into a baby gorilla, rolling around and tapping at his play daddy with gentle affection.

A father, I thought. My friend gave his time at that party to be a dad to my son. His kids were there, but he tuned in to the little boy sitting on the sofa whom he had never met and who needed him, just for that afternoon.

In the wild, a mother animal will take over for an abandoned baby animal with no blood ties. The males won't do that. This is not the case with humans. During those cold months in New York City, what I saw often from my male friends were generous, immediate, and gentle attempts to simulate daddy love where it was needed.

• • •

One mid-afternoon, I was home with Wallace and James and Dad. Dad was on the floor playing "town." When the boys and I first moved in with my parents, my father went to this great toy store, West Side Kids, and bought a set of wooden blocks for the boys, blocks shaped like all the buildings in a small town. Did my father know when he bought the toy how wonderful it was? Well, maybe. I don't think my father did many unintentional gestures in the two years I lived with him between my marriages. My boys had spent a big chunk of their lives growing up in a tiny little town in the Midwest. Their little village was different in every way from New York. It had a bakery, a post office, a school, a barbershop. The little wooden buildings and streets my father so wisely set up in the living room looked exactly like the place my boys had come from, even down to the lettering on the words "Post Office." To play, Dad would fold all six feet three inches of himself down onto the Oriental rug and "drive" the cut-out wooden milk truck back and forth to the "Market" while Wallace and James placed the trees and houses.

"*Vroom, vrooooooom.* Okay, making a delivery. Oh, hello, Mr. Fetcho." (Mr. Fetcho was the name of a butcher we knew growing up.) "I have a delivery of milk!"

"Oh, thanks, Frank." (A made-up name.) "I'll meet you round back!" Dad got into these games. I watched from the sofa. The sounds of this town brought me back to my own childhood, of mornings spent in this same living room with Dad telling Andrew and me his made-up Barbara-the-Gorilla and Bob-the-Bear stories. Barbara lived in the Congo and Bob lived in the American Northwest. They had friends and adventures, and every once in a blue moon, each would travel to the other one's land. It cracked us up imagining a grizzly bear in the jungle, meeting characters like Aloysius, the lion, and his wife, Cornelia.

While I was dreamy with thoughts of children and childhood, watching the boys and Dad play town, my seven-mile stare was broken by the doorman calling up from the lobby. There was a delivery for me.

I waited at the apartment door. There was a mezuzah (a Jewish prayer on a scroll) placed on the door frame by the family who had lived there forty years before. It had been painted over many times by the building, but my mother never took it down and loved having it. "I think it protects our family," she used to say when one of us asked about it. I reached up and touched its smooth edges until the elevator arrived. A man emerged and handed me a garment bag to sign for. None of us was getting many deliveries that February. This was an event. It was like we were on the farm on *Little House on the Prairie* and a wagon had unexpectedly rolled up to the house from Mankato. "Whoa. What's that, Ish?" Dad called out.

"Don't know. I'll be right back."

I went into my bedroom and unzipped the plastic bag. Inside was a beautiful, black, flowy dress with a note.

"Now that you are back and looking so stunning, you may get asked to a party or two. Thought this might come in handy.

All my love, Marina"

Marina is my most glamorous friend. In New York she is revered for her beauty, taste, elegance, and generosity; literally, she is written about in fancy fashion magazines because of these qualities. She's hugely glamorous, well turned out, and witty, but she will also eat the hot dogs at the movie theater and let her kids raise hamsters that end up having a million babies. She is kind. We became friends in our early twenties, and our mothers were childhood friends, so the fact that she is an Upper East Side icon and I felt like an Upper West Side tumbleweed didn't make one ounce of difference to her. She knew the jump from wife-of-a-professor-in-small-town-Ohio to single-woman-in-New-York was a big one, and she was going to help. I had been worried about the clothes thing, and seeing that smokin' dress felt fun, and if I wanted it to, I could choose to see it as hopeful.

chapter 13

When Wallace was accepted into preschool, two important things happened:

1. Wallace was forced to face what was happening to him. (You learn many things in school, including how similar or different your family looks compared to everyone else's.)
2. I had to walk Wallace to school. Walks are always a good idea.

On one of those walks, I ran into Tucker.

Tucker was a boy I had always admired growing up. He is easy to admire. He was the perfectly scruffy, horn-rimmed glasses, shy-smiled guy; too handsome to be described as having "schoolboy good looks," though he *had been* a schoolboy, a prep-school boy. He is about four or five years older than I am, and a stepbrother of friends of mine. Of course, I had never actually spoken to him, maybe once, but mostly I looked at him from afar and thought of the dream world I would have to live in for him to even look my way. He later went to some great school, became an engineer, and married a woman who seemed to be outstanding in every way. She was a doctor. She could be described as an English rose. She had freckles, bright eyes, and looked like she was smiling even when she wasn't. Again, I didn't know them well, but the sight of them made you think of happiness, success, and calm. They looked responsible. I'm sure they were described all the time as "good people."

Writing this feels awful because I wish what happened never happened, but the wife died of cancer when she was thirty-six. The only thing I think appropriate to say about this is that it was very, very sad.

It had been five years since that sad time when I ran into Tucker one slightly rainy midwinter morning. I was pushing Wallace in a stroller down a long side street to his new school. We were both wrapped in wool-and-down parkas. I was trying to protect Wallace from icy, spitting rain with my father's oversized golf umbrella. In Ohio, you just hop in the car. I hadn't prepared myself for New York City stroller life and all the gear you have to have for it. There are elaborate, fitted rain tents you can attach to strollers so you don't have to jerry-rig abnormally large, rather dangerous umbrellas precariously over your young child, but I had left the tent that came with my stroller in Ohio, and it's next to impossible to buy that stroller accessory separately. I was using the umbrella method.

To walk from my parents' apartment to Wallace's school, you have to journey uptown four blocks and then west across

ISABEL GILLIES

four long avenue blocks. This is a part of the Upper West Side
that looks particularly cold and industrial in the winter—like
a little Berlin in New York City. To get a bus to Wallace's school
from my parents' place, you have to walk south two blocks, then
wait, sometimes a long time, for the bus to take you across the
four avenue blocks, then you walk uptown six blocks or take
another bus; taking the bus never seemed worth it. The walk
was a schlep, but it was a schlep Wallace and I did together. I
was singing the song about the letters of the alphabet and about
alligators and balloons from the Maurice Sendak book that
Carole King put to music. I was trying to keep Wallace afloat.

He was miserable. "Where is my dad? Where is my dad?"

He didn't say that out loud, but the serious expression on
his little face told me he was thinking about it constantly. Wallace has the skin of a tulip, he feels everything, and miraculously he can tell you about those feelings, like the mouse in
the children's picture book *Frederick*, and like his dad, who is,
after all, a poet by trade. Nothing is more heartbreaking than
a seriously hurt child deep in thoughts you are helpless to
stop. Nothing.

Just as I was belting out about "*i*mitating *I*ndians!" I looked
up, and there was Tucker.

Our parents are friends, so there was no need for catching
up; we each had a vague idea about what the other one's deal
was. We were in freezing rain, Tucker was going to work, and
I was getting my cold kid to school. We both had big stories to
tell, but we didn't. We exchanged a few obvious formalities and
went our separate ways.

I left him with a feeling: regret. I had a simple regret that

I had not put on lip gloss before I left the house that morning. I had run into someone who in many ways was "the perfect man," and he was as attractive and kind as I had always remembered. The feeling about the lip gloss was a seed. It was as if Tucker had given me a tiny round seed. I planted it into the palm of my hand and held on to it. I wanted to look pretty for someone other than my husband. Something had shifted.

But that was it.

This story doesn't end with Tucker and me falling in love and becoming the answer for each other's big life questions. I think we saw each other one other time on that same street. When I think about how everything fits together, and how everyone you encounter affects the outcomes in your life, I think about Tucker and his misty, horn-rimmed glasses.

chapter 14

My friend Fran, a fiercely devoted mother of three, is on something like year fifteen with her husband. She is also someone who calls and checks in with her friends frequently. One day while Fran and I were on the phone batting around the subject of would-you-ever-go-back-to-him-if-he-wanted-you-to, she surprised me by saying rather forthrightly, "Um, why would you do that?"

"Well, I don't know, because *HE'S MY HUSBAND*???"

"Yeah, I know," she said, adding a bunch of stuff about respecting my decision whatever it was, blah, blah, blah. Then she said, "But, Isabel, wouldn't that be sort of depressing?"

I was actually struck dumb.

"I mean, I know, the boys and everything," Fran went on, "and who knows, and I get it, but isn't it exhausting to think of going back and living with someone who hurt you so badly? Wouldn't it be more fun to, I don't know, do something else?"

With Fran's simple and brave question, I heard a little crack. She was only offering a thought as a friend, it's not like

Fran is God or anything, but maybe the way she said it, or maybe because the moon was in the seventh house, or maybe because she was right, I listened to her. I decided right then that if Josiah ever asked me back, I would not go. (He never did ask, but I wouldn't have gone if he had.)

That's a decision that I have never admitted to anyone, because it felt and still feels like a disloyalty to my boys. In that moment of decision, I understood what Josiah must have felt when he left his commitment to our marriage: heartbreak. My own grown-up heartbreak might have been the crack that I heard. For me, the decision was like the moment in *Titanic* when Kate Winslet decides to leave her frozen love to fall to the bottom of the icy sea, and swim, blowing her whistle, toward the rescue boat. She saved herself. I was going to save myself.

Goodness, I hate admitting that I was walking away from any dream of staying married to my sons' father, because divorce is not what I believe in. It's not part of what I think is the right way to do things. And I never got to know the other side: I never learned what it feels like to rebuild a marriage after something has damaged it. Maybe that rebuilding is the ultimate—the most moral, the most rewarding—in doing what you are supposed to do, but it wasn't in the cards for me or my kids. My sugar basket had broken; it was gone, and although I never in a million years imagined I would, I left all the shards in the garbage can.

I started over.

chapter 15

Almost everybody's a cupid. Thank God. It's part of human nature, isn't it? When one in our herd is without a mate, the cupids emerge. I bet this is the same instinct that makes people cheer for strangers in a marathon.

In New York, one of the best days of the year is the day of the New York Marathon, in November, when almost 40,000 people from all walks of life run 26 miles, starting in Staten Island and ending in the middle of Central Park. Rain or shine, freezing or hot, more than two million non-running people line the streets to wave, clap, and holler to all the runners, as if the runners were their dearest friends or relations. If someone starts to falter, the crowd goes into overdrive cheering for that person. If you wear your name on your shirt, the crowd will call to you by name: "Lewis! You. Can. Do. It!" If they don't know your name, they'll call out the runner's number on your chest. Or they'll use any visual cue. "CHASE BANK! You. Can. Do. It!"

When I first got back to New York, everyone let me settle

in and gave me some time. You would never set up a person whose eyes welled with tears at the mere mention of, well, practically anything. People watched and waited. Remember the seed that Tucker gave me, the lip-gloss seed? It was as if God or someone was watching from above; the second that seed planted itself in my hand, a memo went out to all the cupids in my life—like celestial e-mail—and the phone rang.

First was Marina of the black dress.

"Hi. I have an idea," she said without letting me speak. "He is a friend, an old friend; well, he's not old, I've just known him forever. He's a professor, but don't worry." She was speaking fast as lightning. "He's a professor of money or business or something in New Jersey, but don't worry; he commutes. The only reason he is a teacher is because he already did quite well at his other job. He's young, too, sort of. What do you think?"

"Okay," I said and held my breath.

"Oh, good! Good! He is so nice, and even if you don't fall in love, he is a gentleman and will take you out for a fun evening. It's a perfect way to get back into dating! He won't be a bad guy. I'll give him your e-mail."

E-mail?

It was like a joke out of *The Jetsons*. When I dated before I got married, there had been no e-mail. Maybe some people had e-mail then, but I didn't use it until well after I was married. Now, not only was I going to have to negotiate dating as a mother of two young children (whom I nursed until they were almost two, meaning the bod wasn't what it once was, not by a long shot), but I had to date using e-mail?

"Oh, okay, so he's going to just e-mail me?"

"Well, he might call at first to be polite, but then I'm sure you'll e-mail."

"Wow." I walked into the kitchen, where my parents and kids were milling around, and mouthed, "I'm going on a date."

My parents tried to act casual, but the mood in the kitchen was the mood of parents whose loner daughter has just been asked to the prom. I bet they even went into their bedroom and did the Happy Dance. The Happy Dance is a jig they do together in private when good fortune befalls one of their children, when someone gets into college, is pregnant (and married), gets a job. I have only seen the Happy Dance once—they didn't know I could see them—after my brother announced he was getting married to his girlfriend, Nonie, whom they loved.

In the kitchen, I finished feeding the boys their supper, handed the dishes over to Dad, who had kindly offered to wash them for me, and shuffled behind the boys into the bedroom. While they were slowly pulling off T-shirts and socks (this takes small children twenty minutes to do, but if you worship Maria Montessori like I do, you let them), I looked over at my computer; there was a red dot, indicating that I had an e-mail.

I went over to the computer like Molly Ringwald in *Pretty in Pink* (when she gets that primitive e-mail from Andrew McCarthy on a giant '80s computer in the library) and saw the unfamiliar name, Mark Finner.

Before I popped open that e-mail, I thought of what Marina had said: "He won't be a bad guy."

How did she know? I didn't marry a bad guy. But he did hurt me badly. How did she know that even if this guy wasn't "bad," he still wasn't going to hurt me or my boys, just because he was human? What if I liked him and he didn't like me? That wouldn't qualify him as "a bad guy," but it would still hurt. Was I ready to get hurt? People you love can hurt you. That was the lesson I was learning. I can't stand the whole good guy, bad guy division. Everybody is everything and everybody hurts each other. I was at a dating disadvantage at that moment because I was already hurt and sensitive, plus I had two hurt, sensitive little ones hopping around my bedroom. Why would I open that e-mail? Aren't all people pigs (including me, I am sure) who act badly? Doesn't everyone do horrible things—talk behind people's backs and lie and cheat and make mistakes and ruin lives? Why get involved? Really. But I believe in love. Having love is better than not having it. I clicked the mouse.

Hi Isabel,

I just tried to call you but got a voice mail that I don't think was yours. Marina gave me your information and says the nicest things about you. I would love to take you to coffee or dinner sometime if that is something that you would like.

Hope all is well, Best, Mark

I turned around. My boys were tangled up in corduroy and underpants. I swooped them both up in my arms and threw us all on the bed and blew air onto their soft tummies, making tremendous boomer noises, until they laughed so hard no noise came out of their mouths.

• • •

I wish I could write that going on dates was exciting, that funny, crazy things went on, that I had sex in cabanas with Venezuelan Casanovas; but that wasn't the case. That was the case in my twenties (even the Venezuelan Casanovas), but that was well before these days, which had to end early, and which had to involve conservative selections—no drummers, no line cooks, no free spirits (again, the twenties).

I had no ring on my finger. (You might be surprised at the effect the ring has on people. Without the ring, married dads at the preschool told me they looked forward to what I would be wearing the next day. Gross, but I'm not kidding.) But even without the ring, I was, if not married, a marriage kind of person. I didn't want to date. I still thought the deep-purple, electrifying, all-consuming and painful love was the only kind. The love that makes people go to war. The Romeo and Juliet kind of love. That kind of love hadn't ended well for me, a handful of times, but love is love. I have been drawn to it my entire life, and even though I wanted to be wiser, I was going to swing at every pitch and try to change direction. Maybe I wouldn't find Love, with a capital "L," but maybe I would find some other less dramatic kind of love. Maybe civilized, mutual, sustaining love. Socks and shoes love. And maybe that would be real love. Good love. Maybe I didn't really know what I was doing, but I was trying to be very positive about it all.

I read a personality quiz in a popular magazine once, and one of the questions was, "Do you make the same mistakes more than twice?"

As far as men were concerned, yes.

Josiah was not the first guy to dump me. In fact, I was probably dumped more often than not and always by men you might question my going out with in the first place. I'm not saying that everyone who dumped me was a "bad guy"—not at all—but they were not the right match for my approval-seeking, need-to-be-loved personality. I went out seriously and ultimately painfully with three or four of a similar type of man. They even had *almost* the same aesthetic: somewhat like mine but always a bit higher brow. Each of them in one way or another knew about jazz, Brazilian music, John Hiatt, Buddhism, and poetry. Their interests were stimulating, and slightly out of my Pepperidge Farm, Jane Austen, Rolling Stones range. They were different from me. They knew it, too.

Now that I had no time, no money, a shaky self-confidence, and two children, I knew I couldn't mess around (however tempting) with that type of man. Each of them had broken my heart into a zillion pieces. I was dumped on a roof looking out over Seventh Avenue; I was dumped in my own apartment on Greenwich Avenue by a guy who just never called again; I was dumped at an Indian restaurant on Valentine's Day (even though I was wearing a red velvet dress).

I might have broken one or two hearts. Nice guys (think John Cryer as Duckie in the John Hughes movie *Pretty in Pink*). Like an idiot, I dumped them. One of those breakups was because I was still in love with one of the "wrong guys."

But here's the thing: I couldn't get too mad at myself for being involved with so many of these wrong guys, because they were great. Even when they were dumping me in snowstorms on Sixth Avenue, or yelling at me for scratching their Who records, they were pretty fantastic. Yes, my involvement with them reveals how much of a Drama Mama I am, drawn to complication and high stakes. Yes, had I been really paying attention I might have read the signs that they were not as into me as I was to them. Yes, they show how I am sort of like Lily Bart. But something in my shadow side did match theirs, and although the relationships never worked for very long, they did feel good at the time. Riding on the handlebars up Avenue A, waking up to sunrises on beaches in Virginia, coming home from an eight-hour shift working at a restaurant to listen to the entire Simon and Garfunkel in Central Park album while eating pizza in bed. So much good stuff happened with these guys, because no matter what happened between us, they were not actually bad, but good. Luckily, I am still friends with a bunch of them.

I happened to run into two of the "wrong" guys that winter I returned to New York, and we made a dinner date to get together and go over what had been going down over the last few years. These were smart, intuitive men; I guess I was looking to see if their insights into the past had any clues for me.

Ben and Zack were both actors. One was married, one was divorced. We had been in a theater company in our twenties and had spent those twentysomething, fucked-up, climbing-in-and-out-of-each-other's-windows, dazzling years together in New York City, when we loved singing Bob Dylan songs, or listening to entire Sondheim musicals on a record player, quoting the genius, Albert Brooks, watching John Cassavetes movies and drinking beer deep into the night, sometimes ending up in bed (sex), sometimes ending up in bed all together in a pile (no sex).

We were so passionate about everything, it breaks my heart thinking about it. I guess it feels heartbreaking because we were innocent of the adulthood to come. But also, at least for me, those days were about feeding a seemingly unquenchable need for passion, temper, impulsivity, extremes, and hair-raising love. I said then that I wanted to be one of the Cleavers, but my actions were more those of a watered-down Courtney Love. Anyway, the night Ben and Zack and I had a little reunion dinner, we were the grown-up versions of our twenty-two-year-old selves. Endless beer had turned into moderate red wine, the venue was a restaurant instead of someone's studio apartment on a side street in the Village, but our conversation had not lost its passion. We discussed what marriage, love, and children were all about, and instead of referencing Cassavetes, we were talking about our own lives.

"You know, you dumped me, Ben!" I teased. "And actually, you sort of did, too, Zack! Why the fuck am I always the one getting dumped? What's wrong with me?" I literally looked to the two of them for an answer.

I don't think they were surprised that my husband had left me. Not because they saw me as someone pathetic who couldn't keep a husband, but they knew my tendency for losing myself in the romance of a big love with someone who might leave me. They had watched me do it over and over again all through our twenties. They were too nice to say so, but they knew I'd had a hand in inviting the breakup storms.

"Oh, Iz," Zack said, trying to be nice, "we were fucking stupid that we did."

"Yeah, but you did."

"I don't know," said Ben, jutting his hands out in front of him and pausing like he was about to make an important point. "The thing is, Iz, you should go out with someone like . . . someone like . . . like . . . YOU."

He was talking about the side of me I am most proud of. My roll-with-it, be fair, democratic, upbeat self. Fair enough. It would be a good idea to seek someone out who could, like me, walk on the sunny side.

I lay in bed that night half-watching a cooking show, but really meditating about my evening with Ben and Zack. In my twenties, at different times, I had sat on a park bench or stoop with each of them crying my eyes out, describing in detail the multitude of reasons why I loved them and searching for answers to why they didn't want to be with me. I remember Zack trying to listen and take me seriously, but all he really could offer was an observation about how large my tears were. He said they were the tears of a 1940s movie star (which made me love him even more). I remembered the blank, confused look that each of them had had during my appeals. Was it way too much emotion for their kind of twenty-three-year-old boy to handle? How could that be? They were actors; emotion is our thing. They were not swayed by me or by my requests for accountability. *How about that?* I thought in bed, almost out loud. *All I was asking for was love and accountability.*

I remembered, then, when I was up the Saint Lawrence

River for my grandfather's funeral. Funerals up there are simple affairs. The family meets on an island to bury the urn (in my grandparents' case, both of their urns were made by my mother's sister, Jenny, who is a potter) in a small clearing where other members of our family are buried. My father, brother, and uncle dug the hole for my grandfather the evening before. The whole ceremony is like something out of a Faulkner short story; it's beautiful, rural, and hands-on. Anyway, Ben was my boyfriend at the time, and he was doing summer stock. I had asked him the night before the funeral to call me on that day. You would think that that would be a no-brainer, but I had to ask for it, maybe sensing that he wouldn't do it: "Please call me, okay? I think I'll be a little sad and will want to talk."

He didn't call. He never called that day. So I let him have it. I didn't yell at him; I cried. I cried all of those 1940s tears into the phone. He sounded annoyed by the end, and I felt annoying, but was it so much to ask? He was my boyfriend. It turned out that he was having a summer stock romance while I was eating triangle-shaped egg salad sandwiches at the post-memorial lunch. How could I have been in a relationship with someone who was cheating on me?

I had to admit that night as I lay in bed, after dinner with Ben and Zack, that I always got the distinct feeling with these guys that I wasn't a top priority of theirs. But why? I was just as busy as they were. In fact, I was in college (at NYU) AND pursuing an acting career while they had opted out of college to pursue their careers (which, by the way, was probably a good move for them, as they both have had really interesting, amazing careers). How could I be in relationships with people who made me feel like a low priority, like they had tons of other things to do, when it could be argued that I was just as busy, if not more so than they were?

Maybe I asked too much?

I lay there beating myself to a pulp for being too demanding and needy, but then I thought: *It's not unreasonably demanding to want your boyfriend to call on your grandfather's funeral day.* The men I was picking were saying they wanted love and me and to share, but did they? In retrospect, and maybe even at the time, it didn't seem like it, at least with me. Were there men out there who could have handled what I was dishing out? Maybe those men were not at the Tisch School of the Arts but down the street at the Stern School of Business. Maybe if I had chosen one of the business school students instead of hottie actors and tattoo artists named Tragedy (true), I wouldn't have been lying in bed trying to figure out what had gone so wrong; maybe I would be lying in bed next to my husband of ten years.

I must have needed all those storms, but why? My head was spinning. I felt like Scarlett O'Hara; she always seemed so confused, could be weepy, had a temper, loved her parents, fell hard in love with the wrong guy, made dresses out of curtains, questioned why she ended up where she ended up, and then figured it out. I had to figure it out, but it was late at night, and anyway, I had tomorrow.

chapter 16

Ben was the first guy to dump me, actually, when I was twenty-one. He was electrifying on stage, slightly grungy in that 1990s Eddie Vedder kind of way, and dead sexy (as my mother would say). Distant but sexy. We listened to music, cooked clumsy meals of sweet potatoes and huge pork chops, saw endless movies at the Film Forum, stared into each other's eyes on his rooftop, and went to Greece in a sort of *The Sun Also Rises*, sitting-around-in-cafés-being-in-love-and-feeling-European kind of way, then it fell apart and he dumped me. I was destroyed. I wallowed, cried, and wandered the streets looking for him; I bugged his friends when I couldn't find him. I indulged in the deep-red, bloody hurt of it all. After months of hearing about "BENNNNNNN," my mother—because (a) she couldn't take it anymore, and (b) she almost always says or does something wonderful whenever something makes me sad (it's one of her most beautiful qualities; that and how she never wants anyone to be cold)—offered to pay for a therapist.

Going to a therapist felt like getting a first apartment or even walking to the store by myself for the first time when I was ten years old. I was taking on responsibility. I was going to explore my anguish by myself with a doctor. I was going to talk about Ben until I was blue in the face and figure out why he had left me and why I was in so much pain about it.

Dr. C's little first-floor office looked like an Upper West Side shrink's office out of any movie you have ever seen: white walls; brown flat couch; an ethnic, braided wall-hanging on one wall and bookshelves on the other. There was a stark dollhouse in one corner, where children could play out their experiences of family, and a box of Kleenex next to a lamp. Dr. C reminded me of Gloria Steinem because of her glasses and in no other way: as with most good shrinks, I knew very little about her, but Dr. C seemed to me to be soft-spoken and a bit timid.

I sat cross-legged on the brown, flat couch and immediately started going over every detail of how Ben and I had met at my twenty-first birthday party, which Sasha (my roommate at the time) and a short-lived boyfriend of mine (an earnest, sweet drummer) had thrown for me. I told Dr. C as fast as I could and in great detail about Ben's sensitive, artistic soul and his messy brown hair and how he cheated on me with a really good stage actress at summer stock. I painted the most colorful and detailed picture of my hopeless, Wagnerian love for him. How could I survive without him? I held the box of Kleenex in my lap throughout the session.

Dr. C listened, then quietly asked about my mother. I countered with more stories of Ben. Road trips to Maine (a place I adore and he really didn't care for—hello, red flag), our shared artistic goals, his cool mother whose name was Shelly, our trip to Greece! How could Dr. C ignore a trip to Greece where we listened to David Bowie and slept under the stars in a park? She would nod, listen, then ask about my mother. What about my pain from the breakup? I wondered. What about how I stood for hours on a street corner in midtown, looking up at his apartment?

Nope. Mother.

Did I mention that I wanted to marry him?

Nope. Mother.

Will it interest you to know that I feel like DYING because I miss him so much?

Nope. Mother.

Not only did she want to know about my mother, but she wanted to know about my mother's mother, and even the mother who came before that. Dr. C was the first person to call to my attention the importance of mothers. Having since lived with my mother while being a mother myself, I now think it IS all about the mother. But I didn't get it then.

This is my mother: She has all the right sauces, all the right herbs. Even on the most run-of-the-mill Thursday night, if there is lamb for dinner, there will be mint jelly, and if there is ham, there will be good French mustard, and probably spoon bread. A green salad has minced chives, and a bowl of soup will have a crunchy cracker served alongside on a plate. My mother's meals never seem to be a big production; she stealthily thinks through the preparations in advance so everything you might need will be right there. She stocks Mallomars in the larder in the fall, homemade preserved lemon in the fridge in the winter, and a pitcher of lapsang souchong tea with real mint at all times in the summer (she will pour chilled glasses of the tea and bring them to the lawn-mower guy along with a cookie that she also baked that day); if she has to get up at five in the morning to do it all, so be it. Her details are hints that she is there and loving you.

When Wallace was born, we lived ten blocks away from my parents. I don't remember my mother in our apartment holding the baby as much as I remember the meals she made us and left with the doorman. I don't say that in a bad way. Well, maybe a little; I would have loved to lie around with her and stare at Wallace. But it might have been easier for her to nourish us once removed. I get the impulse. Josiah himself cooked elaborate chicken dishes when Wallace was born. And after James was born, I formed an obsessive habit of making granola and sending piles of it to Josiah's brother, who was serving in the Iraq war. I don't blame anyone for cooking rather than sitting with an infant. Preparing food can be a way of being close but not too close. But sometimes, instead, we need someone to sit there with us, and not worry about the meal.

My mother's mother wasn't close enough to her. There is a story about my mother at age thirteen taking the train from Croton-on-Hudson, where she lived, to go to New York City to buy her school clothes—by herself. How lonely does that sound? Where was her mother? I think my mother compensated for what happened to her by never for one second leaving us to feel uncared for, unaccounted for, unprepared for. She may not sit with us and just hang out for hours on end (that is for me to do with my kids; it's an evolution), but if I needed a dish for a Bedouin feast at school, she made it; if I needed a permission slip signed, it was there in blue ink in the morning; and if I needed clothes for school, she was by my side.

As I grew, it seemed easier for my mother to spend time with me, especially if there was a point to what we were doing. When I was in first grade, she took me down to Little India to get an authentic sari so I could present my report on India dressed in something traditional. I was beside myself. We took the subway together, just us, to somewhere exotic and out of the way of our usual hunting grounds (probably the East Thirties); there, we huddled in a little storefront filled with shelves upon shelves of intensely colored silks, while an Indian woman wrapped and draped me. I remember my mother, in her tweed suit and knee-high boots (her work clothes), sort of jammed between a ladder and the wall so as not to get in the way of the great swaths of cloth being measured. Almost like a balloon slowly floating out of an absent-minded child's grasp, her hand reached up to feel a peacock blue sari. The way she admired it made me think she wished that she could put it on just for a day. Maybe she wished she lived in India, or could go to India. Maybe she wished the fitting was for her. Maybe her mother didn't think about her school projects or the details. Maybe her mother never took her on a subway ride downtown, just the two of them. Maybe Dr. C was right. Maybe it is not only about the mother, but the mother of the mother, and the mother of the mother's mother before that, and so on back in time.

I don't know how this works if you're adopted, but for the rest of us women, there is often a truly electrifying, surreal moment when you suspect that you are turning into your mother. I look so much like my mother these days that I should probably check us into a Columbia University study on genetics, but that doesn't throw me nearly so much as the vivid moment when I behaved like my mother: That kicked me in the pants. That moment came recently when I realized I had walked eight blocks out of my way to get cilantro, at just the right store, to eat with the chili I had made for dinner. I know no one would have noticed if we had no cilantro, or if we'd had cilantro from the store just a block from our apartment. Furthermore, I knew the children would pick it off their chili. They wouldn't even eat it. But I was driven by my mother's voice in my head.

I argued with that voice all the way up Broadway:

Me: Just get in the subway, it's getting dark, you
    are carrying bags, who cares about the stupid
    cilantro?
Mother: It will taste marvelous. It's worth it. It's fresh,
    and chili needs it to wake up a bit.
Me: How moronic. Being a good mother has nothing to
    do with herbs.
Mother: Oh, you would be surprised. Details make things
    taste good. Details show you care.
Me: The boys won't notice.
Mother: It will be worth it and won't take but a second.
Me: Go home and see the kids or you are a bad mother.
Mother: They will notice the cilantro somewhere in their
    soul. They'll be glad they have a mother who makes
    an effort. You are NOURISHING them.

Me: Taking care of children is more about hugging than cooking!

By the time the struggle in my head reached this peak, I was at the market. So what the hell. I marched in and grabbed a bunch of cilantro. The urge to be perfect, or thorough, or maybe just thoughtful, like my mother, is strong.

chapter 17

I borrowed a friend's shoes for my date with Marina's friend Mark, because that was the biggest hole in my Ohio wardrobe. They were golden and slinky and just one size too big; I thought I could swing them for the night. Wrong.

I don't even remember what Mark Finner looked like. I really don't. I know he was attractive, fit, and Jewish. He took me to a good fish restaurant on the Upper West Side. He was a proper grown-up, had made a reservation and secured a lovely little table in the corner.

We had decided to meet there. He had offered to pick me up, but I thought, no, getting there on my own steam would be the right thing to do. I decided to take the bus down Central Park West for two reasons. One, because the restaurant was on Columbus, which is one block over from Central Park West. The walk over from where the bus stopped would take me past the American Museum of Natural History. Not only did I spend most afternoons there with the boys, so it reminded me of the two most important members of my team, but it's just stunning at night; the planetarium glows blue, and you can see all the planets through the glass building. The metaphor that I was a tiny component in this great universe of ours was obvious. My date that night, looming and intimidating to me, was small in the grand scheme of things. Perspective. Perspective.

The other reason to take the bus was because I could read a section of the *New York Times*, which not only would be good because it's useful to read the paper, but also would distract me, and if Mark saw it in my pocket maybe he would think I was smart, or practical, or just a Democrat.

As soon as we were seated, we ordered drinks. Mark ordered a big scotch on the rocks and I ordered white wine. Just before the drinks arrived, I decided I should go to the bathroom before conversation really started.

Here comes the problem with the one-size too big shoes. They had made walking difficult on my way past the museum. Not only had I strained my calf muscles trying to keep the shoes from slapping and wobbling, but I had tripped a couple of times—once getting off the bus and once rounding the corner to the front door of the restaurant. Our lovely corner table was far across the room from the *steep* staircase that led to the bathroom; sitting across from my first ever date since my husband had left me, I took in the well-polished wooden floors, and I started to panic.

"Well, you want to know what?" I said to Mark Finner, biting the bullet. "I wanted to look nice for our date, but didn't have any pretty shoes, so I borrowed some from my friend, who dropped them off at my parents' house yesterday. Marina did tell you I live with my parents, right? With my parents and my kids." I looked him right in the eye to see if that made him flinch. "Anyway, the borrowed shoes are too big and I think I'm going to fall when I walk across the floor," I said, and he smiled.

"Well, if you do, I promise not to laugh."

I made it to the bathroom and back, but on the way back he looked at me like, "Watch out there," so I had created a little inside joke.

We decided to share a chopped salad and then I ordered grilled shrimp and he had the salmon. Unfortunately, but probably naturally, I talked and talked and talked about my ex-husband.

It turned out that Mark Finner was an extremely prominent businessman. In the middle of our dinner, a twenty-five-year-old-looking guy came over and congratulated him.

"It didn't seem like you knew him," I said, trying to be neat about my couscous.

"No, I didn't, I—" He looked embarrassed.

"Are you famous and I just don't know it?" I said.

"No, no, I just ended my job today. I was in finance," he said.

"I don't really know anything about money."

Sometimes I say true enough statements such as, "I don't really know anything about money," trying to seem honest by playing dumb and, maybe even one step worse, trying to be charming using something that I am insecure about. I knew about money. I had been managing my own finances and the finances of my little family for years. I had paid the bills, saved, spent, gotten nervous about it, thought it didn't mean anything compared to some things, then thought it meant everything. I don't like to talk about it, but I know about money. However, because my first date after my marriage had fallen apart was terrifying, I employed that slightly unattractive habit one more time.

"That's silly. Why don't you know anything about money?" he said, calling me out.

"Well, I do, I mean, I pay all the bills and I make money sort of, did Marina tell you I am like the tenth banana on a TV show? I just don't know about how money works in the world. Stocks and things."

"Well, here is what you should do about that," he said. "Think about a company you like. Right now."

"Um, okay. Whole Foods?" A Whole Foods Market had opened up at Columbus Circle in New York while I was in Ohio. In fact, Columbus Circle and its surroundings had transformed completely while I was in Ohio, from a dump in the middle of the city into a shiny center of commerce. The reconstruction symbolized for me how much can happen when you are not looking, plus I had thrown up in a Whole Foods in Cambridge, Massachusetts, when I was pregnant with James, and I always thought it was funny how a market famous for healthy food had literally made me sick. I spat it out: "Whole Foods."

"Yes. That is a good one. Whole Foods. Tomorrow, look in the index of stocks in the business section. You do know that that *New York Times* of yours"—indicating my paper that was jammed into the seat—"has a business section, yes?"

"Yes," I said and crossed my eyes.

"Well, go find Whole Foods and see how that stock is doing.

Then go to the Internet and read everything you can about the company: who runs it, if it is doing well, and why or why not, and then follow your stock every day. I would suggest that you could buy a share or two to make the game more interesting, but you don't have any money, do you?" He said it in a wise way, not a jerk way.

"No. I really don't," I said.

And that was that. He dropped me off in a taxi, didn't kiss me, not even on the cheek, but thanked me for the lovely evening and rode off to his bachelor pad on the Upper East Side.

•   •   •

"Uno, dos, tres, CHO. Uno, dos, tres, CO. Uno, dos, tres, LA. Uno, dos, tres, TE! Cho-co-la-te, Cho-co-la-te, bate bate, Cho-co-la-te!"

This was a little song that Erica taught to the boys. It's infectious, and once it starts, the entire family will sing it all day long until someone fearing for their sanity demands its termination.

"Uno, dos, tres, CHO. Uno, dos, tres, CO. Uno, dos, tres, LA. Uno, dos, tres, TE! Cho-co-la-te, Cho-co-la-te, bate bate, Cho-co-la-te!"

The morning after my first date in almost a decade, the winter morning's sun was streaming in the windows, and all anyone could hear in our apartment was *"Uno, dos, tres, CHO. Uno, dos, tres, CO. Uno, dos, tres, LA. Uno, dos, tres, TE! Cho-co-la-te, Cho-co-la-te, bate bate, Cho-co-la-te!"*

Even though absolutely nothing had come of it, not even the tiniest of sparks had been flung into the air, I was in a good mood. I had accomplished going on the date. When I heard the noises that told me my parents were up (who could stay asleep while a grown woman and two little boys sang the "*bate bate*" song?), I bounded into their room to report on the evening.

"Oh, good!" my mother said upon my entry and got back into bed in her wrapper. My father was still in bed reading the *Times*.

"Well?" my mother said, bright-eyed, awaiting the play-by-play. I sat on the end of the bed.

"It was good," I said confidently. "He was nice."

"What did you order?"

To my mother, what someone has to eat is the most important piece of information to obtain, regardless of the occasion.

"We shared a salad. Then he had salmon and I had shrimp," I said.

"Good . . . Delicious." She nodded. "And . . . what's he like?"

"Well, he's serious. He's sort of no nonsense. He gave me an assignment to look up a stock," I said, reaching over to find the business section.

"Oh, yes, he's a teacher? Is that right?" my mother probed.

"Yeah, I guess. But I think he retired, which I think is weird because he really isn't that old."

"What did you say his name was?" my father asked.

"Mark Finner."

"Yeah," Dad said with a smile on his face. "He did retire, from Goldman Sachs."

"Yeah, that's right, and you know what? Someone he didn't know came up to him during dinner and congratulated him."

"Well, I bet they did. He made two hundred fifty million dollars yesterday," Dad said, pointing to the article, then tossing the business section of the paper to me.

"I hope he paid for dinner!"

Sometimes in my marriage to Josiah, we fought about money. I remember once yelling, "Fine! I wish I could start all over and marry a billionaire!" Histrionic, silly, and not nice. If I had ever imagined I actually would have to go back to New York, I wouldn't have yelled it. But I had a habit of letting what I said get out of control, which kind of felt good, until I truly hurt someone's feelings, and then it really felt bad.

But now I was in New York, in the first years of the twenty-first century. Billionaires were around. The actress Ellen Barkin had just been left by that billionaire guy; it was all over the papers. Maybe I would marry him? I mentioned that to Dad once and he said he wouldn't allow it. It was a joke conversation, but he wasn't joking. Money is tricky, and it's stupid to think that you don't need it, but marrying for it is stupid, too. It's a balance, I guess.

Indeed, Mark had paid for dinner. My father, my mother, and I were all amused that my first date had been with Mark, then I got up to make breakfast for the kids. I knew Mark wasn't going to call me again. I wasn't his type and he wasn't mine. And I wasn't quite ready to date, but Marina had been right, Mark had been a gentleman and a good way to "get back into it." Also, I had an assignment to learn a bit more about how money works, something I needed to do. Everyone has value; you just have to know what to take away.

chapter 18

Even though heartbroken, I was quickly getting into the habit of not living with Josiah. I had even gotten into the habit of doing the thing I hated most to do alone: the bundle. During the 1700s in Colonial New England, there was a practice called "bundling" that was used during the courtship of a man and a woman before marriage to assess whether or not there was compatibility (without having sex, of course). The young couple was put to bed together for the night; to prevent them from doing it, a dividing board was placed between them, or one of them was tied into a cloth bag called a "bundling" bag. I love this bundling idea, and think actually you could suss out whether or not you could be close to someone for a long time just by being wrapped in a bag alongside them all night. I bet a lot of compatibility in bed and elsewhere is about how you breathe or smell or what noises you make. I am not at all sure you have to actually have sex for your brain to understand if it is a go with another person or not. Plus, maybe you could whisper and chat like kids at a sleepover until you both drifted off. Sounds lovely to me, even if it is a little puritanical and weird; I do come from those puritanical people, after all. But I am talking about the other kind of bundling right now, the parka kind.

When Josiah and I were together and living in snowy Ohio, boy, did we bundle. There were snowsuits and hats, mittens and backup pants, and scratchy scarves around the whole enchilada. Bundling is a pain in the ass, it's necessary, and it takes forever. When Josiah was leaving me, I swear I almost said, "But who is going to do the bundle with me?" The thought of doing it alone made me want to wither into a raisin or never take the boys outside again. But the deal with boys is that they HAVE TO go outside. It was my rule that I had to at least be out somewhere by 11:00 a.m. every day. All of us dressed, all of us ready for whatever might be waiting outside.

To make "the bundle" possible at my parents', I tried to be organized. I had two baskets for outdoor gear in the front hall, and I would weed through these every day. The wet hats went to the dryer, the old socks came out of the boots. But the baskets always looked like two piles of unsorted madness. And organization was only half of the problem; with two boys under five, the process of getting out the door was like trying to keep marbles on a table. Even with cheerful encouraging, neither of them could put the clothes on by themselves. Inevitably, while you are trying to boot up one, the other has gotten hot and itchy in all the wool and has started taking things off. One of them will try to fish out the well-planned snack that is in the bag on the back of the stroller, but the weight of the little arm pushing into the bag will cause the stroller to fall backward. (My fault. Too much weight from my brother's

1970s Matchbox cars I said they could bring.) When the stroller crashes down, both boys will cry. While you recover briefly from that, the water bottle that has been unscrewed without you knowing it will spill. Then cleanup has to happen. But by now you are hot and annoyed in your parka that you stupidly put on too early in the process. You might say "Goddamn it!" and that will upset the boys and will upset you, too, because you lost your cool. To put a cherry on top of it all, your parents are watching from the living room, wanting to help but staying away because when you shouted, "Goddamn it!" you also shouted, "I've got it! It's cool. Don't worry!", trying to keep them at bay, though, really, you do need some help.

The waiting chairs were how I solved the single-parent bundle.

My mother had two little chairs that must have been her mother's. I know she sat on them as a child. One was a small rocking chair, two feet high at most. The other was an even smaller rounded wooden chair. My brother and I sat on them and drank ginger ale in the living room while my parents had evening cocktails. I took them out of the living room where they lived and put them in the hallway.

"Boys, these are waiting chairs. When we are getting ready to go out, you sit on them while I get the mittens and the boots. You HAVE to sit there. You can't get out until I say so. Okay?" I looked down at their little jam-smeared faces.

Wallace nodded. James tootled over to the smaller chair, sat down, looked at me, and gave me the thumbs-up. (James had two really funny things he did as a toddler: one was that he constantly gave you the thumbs-up, and the other was that if he was really mad at you he would call you a "pument." It was his worst swear word. Once, when he was really, really mad he called me a "stupid pument.")

I felt relieved and helped by the waiting-chair system because two little boys quietly sitting in antique miniature chairs was far better than the physical chaos I had previously been dealing with on a daily basis. But the waiting chairs didn't solve everything, because it wasn't just mittens and snow pants that were troubling to do alone. I felt abandoned and left with ALL the questions my kids had: Why did we come here? Where is Daddy? Why do I have to start a new school? Why can't I hold my breath forever? Where did the trees come from? I had to reverse every bad mood, change every diaper, run every bath, come up with every plan.

I was, basically, the captain of the ship. Parenting is scary, even with a partner, because how can any of us truly know how to do it? There are so many pitfalls and complex calculations you have to make, never mind remembering to put on the sunscreen. It takes a minimum of two people to field all the questions. When you do it alone, at least for me, and especially at the start of the journey, it's like living on a wing and a prayer. "Please let me do the right thing," I would pray. "Please let me be strong enough to take their sorrow on myself and show them joy when they cannot see it. Please."

You can get used to single parenting, though. It doesn't take long to start to enjoy being the only one who has the answer. You have all the control, and control is what a lot of people like. You have to be careful not to become an island. I actually didn't make up that idea. About two weeks after I had returned to the Big Apple, I ran into a single guy friend I had known since we were teens. I briefly told him my story and he had said, "Wow, a single mother. Well, watch out for becoming an island. All you single mothers are like islands."

One day, I was lying on my bed with the boys, reading a book about dinosaurs before their bath.

"Mama, what happens when you die?" said four-year-old Wallace.

"Umm."

"If you die, do you never come back?"

"Uhhh."

"Will I ever die?"

"Oh—"

"Will you ever die?"

Oh, my God. I thought maybe I should cover the little one's ears so he didn't start to wonder, too. I thought, *Am I an ID-IOT?* Why would I willingly choose to read them a book about dinosaurs? All of the dinosaurs died, and every book on the subject says so. Every one of them. And who knew that when that question came, it would be followed up by so many other hard-driving questions?

"Oh, sweetheart, well—"

God. Should I bring up God and heaven now? I want them to believe in God and heaven, but what if it's the wrong time? But if not God and heaven, then what? Science and dust and aloneness and death in the cold ground?

"Josiah? Will you come here, please?" I would have called in my old life. I suppose I could have picked up the phone, but that felt weird at that moment.

Just as I was about to flip out, Dad poked his head in the doorway.

"Dad! Oh, thank God. Dad, Wallace was just asking about death," I said, widening my eyes.

"Wallace, well, that's an okay thing to think about," Dad said cheerfully. "Dying is what happens to people when they get so so SO old, like this." Dad started to hunch over and pretend to have a cane. This made me and both boys laugh.

"You get very, very old and very frail." He was talking in an "old man" voice. "Then you get so old that maybe one day your heart just gets too old and it stops. And then you are a spirit and you go waaaay out into the universe—" He rose up and opened his arms wide. "And become a part of everything. Like those dinosaurs."

"And you go to heaven and see everyone you love and who loves you," I said. I couldn't help myself; I wanted Wallace to believe in heaven. I still make myself feel better about death by thinking I am going to meet Bach and see our old dog Angus.

"Is Mama going to die?" he said.

"No, not for a long, long, long time," I said, and prayed that that would be true.

"Am I going to die?" he said, not scared.

"No, my love, not for a long, long, long time," I said, and prayed even harder that that would be true.

"Okay."

"Hey, guys," Dad said to the boys. "Let's get in that tubby. Mumma, you can just take a break for a minute." Dad gave me a smile and took the boys to the tub.

chapter 19

It was time for Josiah to come see the boys for the first time.
He didn't have anywhere in New York to stay, and I didn't
want the boys to go anywhere. At drinks, I broached the subject with my parents like a junior in high school who had just
crashed the family station wagon.

At this point in the time when I was living with them, the
subject of my ex-husband rarely came up. I didn't want to speak
negatively about him (and I really tried not to—to anyone),
and I didn't want anybody to speak negatively about him ever,
but since they didn't have many positive things to say about
him just then, we avoided the entire subject. Admittedly, it
was like living with an alligator in the house and never making mention of him, but that was our unspoken understanding. None of us was in therapy either, so you can imagine the
festering cauldrons of confusion, anger, and frustration inside each of us. But our outsides were calm, cool, and collected,
mostly.

"Josiah is coming to see the boys," I said.

"When?" my mother said, not like she was actually asking, more like she knew this was coming so she was going to get the necessary information and move on.

"I don't know. I thought I should talk about it with you guys."

And without missing a beat or batting a lash, my mother piped up with, "Dad, I've always wanted to go to Chicago. I think we should plan a trip there. Isabel, you should go away with a pal or two and Josiah should stay here with the boys. No sense in them being troubled."

Huh? Chicago? Did she just make that up?

"Sounds right," my father said evenly.

Whoa. This was very strange. How often I felt like I was in a movie in those days. The experience of divorce has so many clichés wafting around it and people *are* similar, no matter how unique you imagine you are. Someone has done everything already and probably made a movie about it. I felt like I was in *An Unmarried Woman, Le Divorce, Kramer vs. Kramer, Heartburn, The First Wives Club, One Fine Day,* and *Sleepless in Seattle* (I know, death is different than divorce, but not entirely).

In *Willy Wonka & the Chocolate Factory*, the boy named Charlie lives in poverty with his parents and all four of his grandparents; every penny should obviously go toward feeding the family. But when Charlie finds a dollar in the street, he uses the found money to buy a chocolate bar. Everything works out for Charlie—inside the candy bar is a life-changing golden ticket; still, risking everything on a chocolate bar was a gamble.

Spending money on a girls' spa weekend felt like buying a chocolate bar with my only dollar; I was using up precious resources that should have been spent on my children. But my mother had told me to do it, and in this who-knew-what-would-happen-next *Thelma & Louise* part of my life, a road trip with women friends seemed fitting. I bet there are thousands of cars filled with women out there, road-tripping around because one of them is getting divorced.

My movie's cast of characters was obvious: me, Bess, Sasha, and Vanessa. Every one of us had small children or was pregnant, every one was too busy to take a weekend off, and every one could have better spent the money elsewhere, but they came to help me in a heartbeat. Even the one who lived in England.

I charged myself with finding the spa. Surprisingly, there aren't a lot of spa possibilities in the New York area. There are very fancy, extremely expensive ones, then an abyss. I did come across one on a Google search that caught my eye because it was called The Emerson. In my twenties, a friend who tended to give me great presents gave me a beautiful old edition of *Three Essays* by Ralph Waldo Emerson. The essays are "self-Reliance," "Courage," and "Experience." From time to time when I feel lost in life, I thumb through the book, and because it is so pretty I have always had it by my bedside. In the months after my marriage ended, not only did those essays help me, but I mused that retreating to a spa and inn called The Emerson might scratch the same itch.

The feeling of being in trouble when you are newly divorced is quite real. You are in trouble. You have to rebuild your life, probably from an emotionally and financially damaged position, and people are angry with you. Divorce upsets people. It disrupts what is "supposed" to happen. People become afraid they might "catch it." They get angry. Not really at you, but sort of. I had friends who argued that no, they were not angry at me, they were angry at HIM. But for me, he was still me and I was still him. I can't imagine being around me was easy. I was tense and defensive. If anyone even questioned a motive of Josiah's or raised an eyebrow at his behavior, I snapped, and I cried very easily. Although I was trying hard to be normal, I had the energy of a rabid animal. My dukes were up and it must have been uncomfortable even for my closest friends.

I felt I was annoying everyone by breaking the good rule of staying married until death parted Josiah and me, and then everything got even more weird and harder for me to get my mind around when the custody sharing of the boys began in earnest, because it was immediately clear that lines would have to be crossed that usually are not.

Josiah's visit to the boys was not the first time I had seen him since I left Ohio, but it was the first time he was going to come sleep in my bed in New York just twelve hours after I got out of it. That is the kind of line I am talking about. That night, when he put his head down on my pillow, my head would have lifted from it twelve hours before. That's divorce. That's the kind of weirdness that everyone has to deal with and adjust for. The abnormal has to become the normal. You have to go with the flow, and if you don't, if you fight the oddity of it all, not only will you get frustrated, but the kids will suffer. You made their lives weird; now you have to conform to all sorts of unimaginable circumstances to make life as good as you can for them.

Josiah's first New York weekend with the boys was the first time they experienced their family as a divorced family. This was the handoff, the explaining where the Children's Tylenol was. Up until that point, their father had disappeared, it was as if he were on a long trip, but now they saw us in the hallway together, awkwardly trying to figure out whether to hug hello or not. They saw us holding back tears and lugging weekend bags through the door.

"Don't worry, angels. Mama will be back on Sunday! You are going to have such a great time with Daddy." My voice quaked and broke and a few tears rolled out. I had to rush out to keep from falling apart in front of them. This was the beginning of what the rest of their lives would look like.

And as bizarre as it was, there was a spa to get to.

• • •

Bess drove. She's a good driver, which I was thankful for. Ever since my marriage broke up, I have had an overwhelming, almost paranoid fear of dying. I can't die. Even if it's not true, I feel wholly responsible for raising my boys, and I can't die until they are well into adulthood. I bet most parents think that, even if they are still married.

Bess, Sasha, Vanessa, and I were headed for the small, hippie town of Woodstock about an hour and a half up the Hudson River from New York City. The trip up to that part of the world is very beautiful, whether you travel by car or by train.

You follow the mighty Hudson all the way. When I was little and we would leave the city in that direction, my mother would always call out as we drove over the bridge at the very northern tip of Manhattan, "Thank you, Rockefellerssss!"

The Rockefellers preserved much of the land west of the Hudson. The land east of the Hudson is a cityscape (it looks like the Bronx, and it is the Bronx for part of the trip), but if you look out the left-hand side of the car as you drive north, you feel like you are looking at the world as it was hundreds of years ago. You see rocky cliffs, forests of trees, and the big, strong Hudson River. The river, bigger and older than you, flows alongside you for most of the ride. When life feels tough or unmanageable, it's good to look at something stronger and older than you are. I'm sure that's why a lot of people in trouble turn to the Bible.

I hadn't been alone with these girls all together since I had become single. We had spoken on the phone, but we hadn't been physically together. There is a big difference (which is why we have to get our heads away from our computers). There are small details that you notice when you spend real time with friends. There are looks in the rearview mirror. There are teases. There are offerings of lip gloss. One of your friends might reach over and get a strand of hair off a sweater or lift up the lid on her bag to reveal a pile of junk magazines. Vanessa had left her one-year-old all the way in England. Sasha was pregnant and had left her husband in the city (pregnant women really shouldn't be away from their husbands; husbands have to find the pizza at 2:00 a.m. and stuff like that). Bess had left her tiny baby and two toddler boys at home with her

husband. Everyone had left a family to be with me the weekend I first had to (and wanted to—oh, how much they needed
and wanted their father) leave my children with their father
because of a custody agreement.

When Bess, Sasha, Vanessa, and I piled out of Bess's car
into Woodstock, it was slushy, gray, and cold. Wrapped in long
sweaters and scarves, the four of us, arms linked, began our
mission to find coziness, food, and purchasing opportunities.
Our first run-in was a store with bubble bath, wind chimes,
and batik headbands in the window. We filed in and immediately started unscrewing the essential oil vials that lined the
counter. Parsley, sage, rosemary, and thyme.

"What brings you lovely ladies up to these parts?" said the
Willie Nelson look-alike store owner.

"We are going to the Emerson Spa," I said.

"Oh, yeah? The Emerson? That place had a big fire last
year. Didn't know they were up and running."

Oh, Lord. But hadn't I made the reservation? Why didn't
they tell me then that the place was toast? I looked at the girls
blankly, and it must have been funny because Vanessa, who
was stoically fighting jet lag, looked at me and started to laugh
so hard. She laughed and laughed, bent over so she didn't wet
her pants. It was contagious.

It turned out to be true that, yes, the new building at the
Emerson Spa had just been finished when it had burned down
the year before, but the "old lodge" was still welcoming guests.
They had booked the four of us in a two-story suite, which had
a small living room with a gas fireplace. Two of us would sleep
on the pullout in the living room and two would sleep in the

double bed upstairs. There were carved, life-sized wooden black bears placed around big heavy wooden beams, wall-to-wall worn-out carpeting, and a deer antler chandelier hanging from the ceiling. There was even a little balcony that looked out on a small, beautiful rushing river, the Esopus.

That night, after our dressed-up, fun, chatty dinner, there was a black pit in my stomach. When all the talk and girl distraction had come to a close, I could feel the anxiety and longing rising up in my esophagus. I knew that feeling; it had begun in the fall and had been inside me ever since. I had been keeping it at bay for weeks. In the bathroom, after washing my face (with someone else's product; half of the fun of a girls' weekend), in a last-ditch attempt to make that feeling stop rising up inside me, I took ten milligrams of Ambien, then I got in bed with Bess. She was on her side, hand on the side of her head, waiting for me.

"Rudy?" Rudy is our pet name for each other. She was asking if I was all right.

I looked at her and shook my head slowly no. She took me into her arms and I cried and cried. I cried as if it were the day he told me he was going to leave. Hearing all that, for the first time that trip, the others floated down in their nightgowns and sat on the side of our bed. It was why they were there, and maybe what they had been hoping for. Waiting for someone to cry can be worse than witnessing the actual act itself. The expressed emotion means it's all flushing through, it's what is natural and expected, like a kid throwing up. No matter how many people go through divorce, no matter how garden-variety the breakup, that loss is unbearable, and friends understand.

I must have drifted to sleep because of the drugs. Bess watched me go and tells me that the last thing I said was, "Rudy, I'll be okay. My ancestors are watching over me."

* * *

We got massages and went on long walks. We window-shopped and drank hot chocolate, all the while solving the world's problems. The last funky store in the Hudson River Valley we visited that weekend was piled high with gorgeous hand-made boots, boots way too expensive to be taken home, but we splayed ourselves everywhere trying them all on. *Moulin Rouge* was playing on the television in the store. Ewan McGregor's intoxicating voice caught our attention, but then the plot of the star-crossed lovers anchored us in for the duration of the movie.

As eleven-year-olds, Bess and I had watched *Gone with the Wind* together in her parents' library. Both of us owned hoop skirts, if you can believe it, and we watched the movie wearing them. We swooned and held hands tightly during almost every exchange between Scarlett and Rhett. We spent hours analyzing that story. How could Scarlett not have seen that Ashley was in love with Melanie? Would we have chosen Ashley or Rhett? Why didn't Scarlett see that Rhett was giving her the world and all of his heart? What made her so dissatisfied? Why couldn't she soften? Was she too mean? How could she love the land more than a person? And then, in the end, the part that crushed our barely adolescent hearts was: We never could get over the bewildering fact that Rhett just walked away. She *did* call for him while she was sick; he had to have believed her, right? How could he give up when she was clearly in love with him, and she was begging him for another chance?

The two twenty-year-old shopkeepers at the store with the cool boots in Woodstock ended up cramming themselves onto the red velvet sofa with us to finish watching *Moulin Rouge*. They didn't seem bothered that we loitered all afternoon wearing the boots and weeping as the young couple in the movie swore they would love each other until their dying day.

• • •

When I arrived home with my weekend bag, Josiah was cleaning up the afternoon snack he had given the boys. He had to go to the airport. Although this was the first time a "weekend visit" had to come to an end for my boys and their father, it was as if Wallace knew what was going to happen. Josiah began the "I'm going to see you really soon" speech and Wallace started crying—screeching. Josiah tried to calm him, as did I, but the boy was voicing what was happening for him and what the rest of us had been skirting around. Why wouldn't you scream for your life to keep your parents from parting ways? He held on to both our hands and tried to pull us together. He was screaming and pulling. Finally, white as a sheet, Josiah tore away and was able to leave me with my inconsolable son. I can't imagine what it feels like to leave your son in the way that Josiah had to that day, but it must be excruciating. What must he have felt on the other side of that door? I sank on the hallway floor, gathering up my little boy. What was he feeling? How bad was it? It seemed bad.

"My sweetheart, it's sad. It's so, so sad that Daddy has to

go away. It's sad for me, too. I feel sad, too. We are the same," I told him with tears streaming down my face. I couldn't make it better for him so I decided to join him and let him know I was doing it. I was going to be emotionally truthful with him from then on and never make him feel like he was off the mark for feeling the way he was. I squeezed him.

"It's going to be okay. It is, my love. It will always feel hard. But you will be okay."

chapter 20

When you are a single mom, Friday nights are a daunting and depressing night to have to survive week in
and week out. However, my old friend Steve, who had not yet
married and was leading a bachelor's existence downtown
(writing novels and poetry by day, going out with other artist
types late into the night), saved me from sweating out Friday
evenings when most of the world was out on a date, even a
husband-and-wife date.

Like a dutiful grandson taking his grandmother to lunch
every Sunday, Steve would show up at my door, politely chat
with my parents (whom he has known since he was twelve) in
the living room while I put the boys to bed, then escort me to a
movie and take me to dinner. At an early hour, he would bring
me home in a taxi, kiss me on the forehead, and take off to
start his real night at a club or party. He did this every Friday.

Steve was not just an old friend. He was *the* old friend with
whom I lost my virginity a very long time ago. We were Romeo and Juliet in age then, but without the intoxicating, ex-

cruciating, passionate love between us. We thought, quite maturely, that since we were such good friends, we should just do it with each other, so we didn't end up doing it for the first time with some more complicated person. We were going to avoid the sophomoric emotional pain that can come along with losing one's virginity.

"I love you," I said, putting a light emphasis on the word *you*, almost a question.

"Well, I love you," he said, using the same inflection I had.

It wasn't "I *love* you." We understood that if you were going to have *sex* and for the first time, love better be involved, and it was, but in an I-think-you-are-fun-and-nice-and-cool-and-I-always-want-to-know-you-so-why-don't-we-just-proceed-with-the-thing-that-can-be-traumatizing-scary-and-awkward-if-done-with-the-wrong-person kind of love.

We never did it again, but, boy, was it a good idea of us to do it (not because it was physically a triumph). I have never looked back at that crucial life experience with anything other than a smile. We were so young, smart, and practical. We remained the best of friends. Steve was the kind of friend who at sixteen took me to the Village on the subway to eat Brie and a baguette at a cafe. He is half Spanish and half American, which makes him mysterious and knowable at the same time. He thinks he has healing hands and many times has rubbed them together and put them on my throat when it was sore and on my head when it ached. He's always been a wonderful friend, so it didn't surprise me that he was there again, but I couldn't have been more grateful.

You might be thinking, Why didn't you fall in love and

marry him? I asked myself the same thing. I am sure my parents asked it the moment Steve and I left their apartment for the movies every Friday night. The notion of falling in love and marrying the "best friend" is a good one, and it's not unheard of. If you are suspicious that you may never find true love again, the next best thing is to join forces with your friend. And there is a good argument to be made that you SHOULDN'T marry for big, deep love, but for solid, trustworthy friendship. I didn't see why I couldn't follow that formula. It would be safe. It would be friendly, and moreover we would be following the same strategy we had put into use when we lost our virginity, and that had worked out great. There was love there, not *love*, but love. And we could probably even have a pretty good time in the sack together if we put our minds to it. But marriage is different. You don't just marry your friend because that's an acceptable answer to a question. Steve and I never fell in love in six seconds.

But right before I fully understood that I would never marry Steve, we went to see *Brokeback Mountain*. My God. Nobody had told me what the movie was about or what it was like. I hadn't read the story the movie was based on, and I had been so out of it that I hadn't read the *Times* Arts and Leisure section in about twelve weeks. I had no idea what I was getting into when we decided to see that movie. The story is about true love and it's about heartbreak. By the end of the movie, when the one cowboy is holding the hanger with his dear love's shirt tidily buttoned up around it by his mother, I thought I would throw up I was crying so hard. Steve was sobbing, too, but I don't know why. Seeing that movie together told me in no uncertain terms that unless I loved like those two men did, I had no business even entertaining the idea of being with Steve, or anyone.

It did also occur to me that even though I was thinking about that kind of passion, maybe I shouldn't go there. I had children to think about. Maybe I should stay strong and single and give them the best I had without a man in the picture. But my father always said you've got to swing at every pitch. I believe he used that baseball analogy when talking about job opportunities or auditioning for school plays—I don't remember him saying that about dating—but I applied it to dating anyway.

There was one guy I was supposed to meet who lived in Greenwich, Connecticut. Sasha's husband had gone to college with him. He was a divorced dad, the father of two kids slightly older than my boys. Dad, good. Greenwich, fine. Step-children, great. I can get down with the suburbs, car pool, and soccer games. Yes, sounds good. Sign me up.

It took a couple of weeks until Mr. Greenwich finally called, and then a few more until we worked out a date to meet (all the while I was stuck in Connecticut mentally, imagining how far away the good public school was from wherever this guy lived), and then, the Sunday that we were supposed to go out to dinner, a *huge* snowstorm hit the Northeast and he couldn't drive in. Never met him.

Not too long after I never met Mr. Greenwich, a friend suggested I go out with an old mutual friend of ours who was still unmarried. He and I knew each other from our twenties, had probably already considered dating and wisely avoided it, yet I let myself get whipped into a frenzy thinking that maybe we had avoided dating earlier in our lives because we were *really* meant to be getting married in our mid-thirties. I imagined us talking and finding out all sorts of things that we never knew before and unlocking the mystery of why on earth we hadn't fallen long ago. We were both dyslexic. He was much shorter than I am, so I bought a pair of inexpensive flats to wear on our first date. (By the way, buying clothes for a date should be put in the bad karma category, along with borrowing too-big shoes. I had long believed that it was bad luck to buy lipstick or a pair of weird glasses for an audition, and don't know why I didn't apply the same rule to my dating life.) I don't think he was thinking as much about our upcoming rendezvous as I was.

As the evening of our date approached, I was in the kitchen with Dad, getting the boys fed and bathed so he wouldn't have to do too much work while he was on babysitting duty.

"What time is he picking you up?" Dad said.

"Uh, you know, I don't know. He hasn't called to tell me yet."

"Oh, well"—Dad was looking at the kitchen clock—"I'm sure he'll call soon, it's almost six." He spoke with the surprise of a gentleman who probably had never made a lady wonder what the plan was.

I went to my computer to see if my old acquaintance had e-mailed. Nothing. Checked the dial tone for a message I might have missed. Nothing. I got the kids into the tub. My mother passed the bathroom and saw me on my knees, washing faces.

"Oh, Loola, I thought you would be getting dressed?"

"Yeah, I think he said he would call a bit later. Maybe he knows it's a hard time of day when you have kids."

She nodded and went to her room. I took the boys out, dried them, shuttled them into my room to put PJs on, and while they did, I called the missing man.

"Hey, I'm not around. Leave a message." *Beep.*

"Oh, Alex, hi. Umm, I'm just wondering if I have the right night"—of course it was the right night, I had had it written down in ink for a week. "No worries, not a big deal, I just want to know if I should put on a dress or a nightgown, heh. Whatever, call when you can. Bye!"

I made those kinds of calls from my bedroom closet. This protected the boys from hearing their mother talk nervously into answering machines, but I also did it because making calls to potential boyfriends was silly and embarrassing. I wasn't sixteen; it felt better to be in the closet. Once I was in there returning a message from Mr. Greenwich when my dad came in to empty the wastepaper basket, his job. "GARBAGE MAN!" he announced as I was trying to be charming on voice mail. As you can imagine, Dad's appearance totally threw me. Having your father see you hunching over, sort of jammed into the shoe rack, in the closet—at age thirty-six—while talking on the phone is almost worse than any embarrassing thing that might have happened in your actual teens.

I took the boys into their room, passing my parents in the living room.

They looked at me like you look at someone who is getting stood up, because I was.

"Want us to read to them?" my mother called.

"Nope! It's all right. I've got it."

I started reading *Curious George*, then I couldn't take it anymore (it's kind of a boring story, but that's not why I couldn't go on); I marched back into the living room and handed the huge yellow book to Dad. "Can you finish this, please? I have to make a call."

My father said, "Sure," and my mother looked up and gave me an air kiss over her *Gourmet*.

Back to the closet. *Ring, ring, ring.*

"Hello?" A whispery male voice answered.

"Alex, it's Isabel. Are we going out tonight or what?" I said, pissed off.

"Oh, yeah, um, what time is it?"

"Seven-o-five."

"Shit. Umm, I just woke up."

"From a nap?" I said, sounding like the mother I am.

"No. It was a big night last night," he said with very little shame.

"Oh, Well, I guess we won't go out, then."

"Um, yeah. No."

I hung up the phone. By the time I went back to the boys' room, my mother was adding another place to the table. "We'll have a nice night at home . . ." She did this thing we all do where you blow air at the other person through your nose, sort of like a horse. It means solidarity.

I nodded, rolled my eyes, and went back to sing the boys to sleep. *No big deal*, I thought, bucking myself up, *better to know that sort of thing now*. But I really had been looking forward to going out to dinner.

There was another blind date, a brother of a friend of a friend. This guy got blotto drinking four gin and tonics before we sat down to dinner and spent the rest of the evening wavering between ranting angrily about his ex-wife and coming close to tears about life without her. I sat at the other end of the table, hoping that some of my advice about how to get back together with her would sink in through the gin. What was the deal? In my twenties, there had been so many amazing men. They seemed tucked in every corner of the universe, and now—now, everything seemed difficult. The men I was meeting had fallen in love and vowed never to leave somebody, only to have it not work out. The weight of the history showed on their faces. They were stressed out, heavyhearted (even if they didn't know it), preoccupied by life details, from their jobs to their kids.

And all those life details were crammed up inside the BlackBerrys that everyone seemed to have in New York. I would come back from the bathroom and the guy would look up at me, but instead of smiling and taking in the fact that I was coming back to the table, he would look down at his machine, push a few buttons, then jam it back in his pocket and try to pretend that he hadn't done whatever it was he had just done and that I hadn't seen him do it. What was he doing? For all I knew he was saying good night to his teenager, closing a business deal, or e-mailing another woman about a date next week. These BlackBerry dates were so different from how I remembered dating from my twenties.

In those days, the young men would be waiting for you to come back from the bathroom. They might have noticed that you were close to finishing your drink and would be talking to the waitress about getting you another one. They would be peeling the label on their beer, staring at your empty chair.

Maybe they would be thinking about the amusing comment you had made just before you got up. They would be listening to the song on the jukebox, waiting for you. They would be waiting for you and doing nothing but that. I think it would be better to come back from the bathroom and find your date kissing someone else at the bar than to find him tapping away on a BlackBerry; more honest. The men I was dealing with now were ten years older and had BlackBerrys. They had built lives and had lost that beautiful quality that youth brings— youth.

chapter 21

Then came our actual divorce.
Josiah and I had signed the separation agreement in Oberlin at the desk of the bank lady in town. That separation paper is a big nail in the coffin of a marriage, but it's not the final one. I had to go back to Ohio to have a judge pronounce us divorced.

I had to go back to our still unsold house and do the I-want-this-you-can-have-that thing. I considered ditching that part. After all, how much can one really want a chair, but I did want the Il Papiro photo albums that I had spent hours and hours assembling and gluing, and a big basket I had gotten at an antiques store in Williamsburg, Brooklyn, called Ugly Luggage; it was shaped like a large "U" and held newspapers. There were two brass handbells that were actually from Josiah's family, but I love bells, and I thought one day the boys could have one each. The way I remembered it, his mother had given them to me, but she probably thought of me as us, and us as him; anyway, I loved and wanted them.

"Well, you just have to do it," my mother had said, as if we were discussing getting a mammogram or cleaning the oven. "It will be beastly, but . . . my poor baby." She gave up trying to give me a pep talk about it.

"I know. Do you think he should pick me up in the car from the airport or should I take a cab?"

"Let's get Dad for that one." She stood up from my bed and went to the living room.

I went to my closet to choose what I would wear in court. I thought of myself in dark blue. Dark blue is such a proper and organizing color. I had a black pleated skirt (which I wished was dark blue) and a cream silk blouse I had bought to wear to Josiah's stepfather's seventieth birthday. I knew my mother had dark blue cardigans.

"Take a cab from the airport," said Dad, leaning into my room.

"Yeah? But it's easy for him to pick me up. He said he would," I said from behind the closet door, holding up my pleated skirt and looking into the mirror.

"Well, it's your choice, but I would take a cab."

"Okay. Thanks, Dad."

The next morning while I was still in bed and the kids were watching TV on either side of me, my mother came into my room in her nightgown.

"Say 'good morning, Granny,' " I said to the boys, who were too absorbed in *Franklin* to notice that she had walked in.

"Good morning, Grannyyyy," they said.

"Loola, I'm giving you this." She handed me an envelope with a heart drawn on it in ballpoint pen.

"It's a Valium," she said, looking straight in my eyes.

"Whoa."

"This is too hard. There are some things in this life that are too hard and this is one of them. You take half of this on the plane and half tomorrow before you go to court. Don't tell Dad. He doesn't approve of drugs, but this will help you."

She was right. It was one of those too-hard moments that just do come along in one's life. I took the envelope, put it down on the bedside table, and sank back into the pillows between the blond heads.

"Thanks, Mumma."

• • •

I bought an eighteen-dollar dark-blue pashmina scarf at the airport. It looked tidy and it would be comforting. I don't know why I wanted to look and be neat about this process, but I did. I tried to appreciate that I could sit in the airport with *Gourmet* without the boys interrupting, but my heart was pounding and I was slightly short of breath. I hadn't even boarded the plane yet. I had called Josiah and asked him to pick me up. I know Dad wanted me to go it on my own, but I wanted a ride from the man himself. We started this together, we were going to end it together.

The one big regret I have in my life was not being at my dog's side when she was put down. Josiah and I had adopted a puppy in Dallas, Texas. We knew nothing about her but that she was alone in the world and needed a home. She was reddish, with a little black on her shoulders, boxy, and had a crinkled-up nose. What she looked like—but we ignored, because we were desperately wanting a little creature to take care of—was a Rottweiler–Chow Chow mix: two of the most aggressive breeds in one little nugget. We named her Cuba. Josiah thought of it; he, like my mother, had a knack for naming. Cuba grew and became our beloved companion, our obsession, our fiercest defender. At two years old, she could no longer be around other dogs and, we feared, any children. One day in Maine my brother David's beloved, innocent little Westie trotted up to the screen door. In a flash, Cuba busted through it from inside the house, ferociously barking and growling, took Harry in her jaws, and shook her head back and forth to kill him. My brother jumped in between them and saved his dog. We grabbed Cuba and took her away to calm down. I held on to her and felt her strong heart pounding: too much, too strong, too fierce. We knew that we had to give her away. I cried and cried in bed. Josiah called farms, shelters, breeders, desperately hoping that there would be a need somewhere for a brave, loyal guard dog. We found a shelter that said they would take her until we found another owner. It was forty miles away. Josiah took her. By the time he got back they had called to say that she was so angry, afraid, and defended that she wouldn't let anyone near her. She was dangerous to people and had to be put down. My sweet girl didn't know where we were. She was confused, and something in her makeup didn't let her handle that confusion and loss in any acceptable way. I have only one other time felt such a raw, unending feeling of loss. There was absolutely nothing I could do to save this animal who only wanted to love and protect me. She was the first animal I ever loved and the only animal I will ever love in that way. The pain was unbearable, inescapable, and instead of withstanding it and going to her so she could die with me, I copped out. I indulged in my grief and fear of death, and stayed at home. She died alone with strangers. I will never forgive myself. Being together when you end a life or a relationship is what is responsible and right to do. I didn't take a cab.

I did, however, take the Valium. My seat on the small commercial plane to Cleveland was in the very first row. During the flight, I read an article in *Vogue* about Dita Von Teese's wedding to Marilyn Manson. I think that marriage is over now, but at the time, I thought how lucky they were to be stepping into a new life, even if they always had to wear black clothes and bizarre makeup. When we had twenty minutes left in the air, I took out my mother's envelope with the blue ballpoint heart on it.

"Excuse me," I said to the one flight attendant. "May I please have some water? I need to take a pill."

He was a young guy with very neatly combed, jet-black hair.

"Certainly," he said and smiled at me.

"Thanks. You see, I am going to get divorced. I mean, I'm getting divorced in front of a judge tomorrow, but tonight I am going to my old house with my husband; well, he is the one I am getting divorced from, but I guess—well, I am sad about it and nervous—"

He must have seen this kind of thing before. People have to fly for all sorts of sad reasons, and flying itself makes people worried, frightened, and upset. He handled the next moment beautifully and spoke calmly.

"Who would let such a pretty girl go? I'll get your water. You will be okay." He went to get the water. There was something about his lovely, calm voice and the half a pill in my palm that was going to take away the feeling that I was falling that really did relieve me. He came back, gave me the water, and said, impossibly, "My name is Angel."

• • •

I don't want to sound like an advertisement for drugs, and I have only taken one Valium in my life, and it was over two days, but, boy, did it work. It took away the feeling that I was going to have a panic attack. Or maybe I *was* having a panic attack, but it enabled me to walk down the street and speak in full sentences.

• • •

I was surprised to find that Josiah wasn't living in our home. I figured it out because our cats were not there. They were "at a friend's," he said. They were clearly at Sylvia's apartment, which was obviously where he was living, but I didn't get that then. (Sometimes I can be so thick.) I was sad that I wasn't going to see our cats, especially Lucas, who had slept every night in the space between my chest and knees when I curled up. If I hadn't been on Valium, missing the cat would have enraged me at first, then sent me into uncontrollable tears, disabling my ability to sort through throw pillows. This is the kind of experience my mother knew was out there for me to endure. She knew there would be something unexpected and painful to deal with, and she wanted to protect me from it. I have no idea what Josiah was feeling, but I was feeling smooth.

I didn't recognize the town that had been my home just a few months before. As we drove through it, I thought it looked like a made-up place, as if I were in a Tom Petty video. When we walked into our wonderful brick house, the smell of the one-hundred-year-old wood hit me. I thought, "Wow, this is the saddest thing I have ever done." Josiah didn't know why I was being so uncharacteristically cool and collected; it probably added to his sense that we had become strangers. We slowly divided up the remainder of our life together. We stood across the island in the kitchen and talked tersely about china. Even though I was on half a Valium, it didn't escape me how clichéd it all was and how sad. We even went to dinner together at the Chinese restaurant we had always gone to. I ordered shrimp and snow peas, which was what I always ordered. He might not have eaten anything, I can't remember, but I do know that he left before the meal was over, not in a mean way; maybe it was all too much. I stayed and finished my supper by myself in a daze.

I spent the night at the Oberlin Inn, which sounds charming, but which is just a two-story motel, five minutes down the road from the house that I no longer shared with Josiah. I went through the motions—bath, brush, TV, read—in a stunned, Valium-numbed haze; then, at last, I fell asleep.

The next morning it was snowing. Not heavy, debilitating snow, but light, beautiful snow. Snow like tears when you are crying from joy. You don't feel the tears; they just fall out of your eyes. This snow wasn't doing anyone any harm; it only fluttered down. Josiah picked me up in our minivan and we drove to Elyria, where the courthouses were.

Even in this poor county in Ohio, the courthouse looks

like a proper courthouse, not unlike the courthouses in downtown New York, judicial and formidable. It even had impressive
white columns. We met our one lawyer on the second floor of
the building, in the hallway. Josiah took off his coat; I saw he
wasn't wearing a suit. So strange. He didn't ordinarily wear a
suit during the day, but during the time he was looking to buy
my engagement ring, every once in a while, he would wear a
suit. I would look at him like "Wha?" and he would smile, shrug
his shoulders, and go off to some jeweler.

Sitting on a wooden bench seven years later in the family
court in Elyria, he was dressed as if it were a normal day. He
looked at me in my carefully planned, pleated black skirt and
said, "I should have worn a suit." Neither of us was wearing a
wedding ring.

My heart ached. My voice was taken away. The abstract
idea of getting divorced was familiar to me by then, but the
reality—the appointment, the bench, the lawyer with his files,
my estranged husband—felt otherworldly, out of my grasp
and all wrong. My mind tried to catch up to the event, but
failed. Our lawyer said, "Okay, guys, we will go in, then the
judge will come in. This judge was once a Marine. Just answer
his questions and we'll be done. I'm sorry about it." It couldn't
be fun being a divorce lawyer.

The courtroom looked like any courtroom you might imagine. There was a bailiff. Our lawyer wasn't kidding about the
Marine part: This judge was huge and intimidating. He was
upright in his robes and leaning forward on his fists. His desk
was much higher than where we were standing.

"Do you two know why you are here?"

"Yes, sir."

"Mrs. Robinson, do you want to get divorced?"

No. No, I don't, sir. Please don't divorce me.

"Yes," I meekly said.

"Mr. Robinson, do you want to get divorced?"

"Yes, sir," he said respectfully.

There is probably a script judges have to follow with people who are getting divorced and I guess he said those things, but he sounded disapproving and disgusted. I didn't blame him. I, too, thought that parents shouldn't get divorced. Even if it turns out all right for everyone in the long run, they probably shouldn't. It's such a gamble.

Our lawyer said good-bye to us and took the stairs down while we waited for the elevator. We walked back into the gentle snow, got into the car, and both cried into our hands.

• • •

What can I say about the violent act of getting divorced? If you have to do it, once it's over, you will feel better. Or I did. Yes, frightened, yes, sad—yes, yes—but also better. You are done. You can move on—legally, mentally, and with a free heart. My divorce was quick, and that was only because Ohio rewards its citizens with a shortcut if you can hammer out the agreement without fighting. Of course, the law doesn't say "without fighting," but that's what it means. Long, drawn-out divorces seem dreadful to me in a thousand ways, and I don't know if the custody arrangements and what-you-get-to-keep outcomes are so different if you get divorced in three weeks or three years. Everybody has to give up more than they want to, and if you have children you are still looking into the future of navigating the shoal-filled channels of shared custody. My advice here is: Be generous, compromise, and be good to each other.

Later that day, back in New York, walking up Central Park West, I felt released. The avenue was wide, full of promise and people, and above it all, the sun was shining bright. A big cliché is coming into my head right now. It's such a big one I hesitate to write it, but I will.

You only do live once.

part
IV

chapter 22

Every month the children's father would fly to New York to spend the weekend. My parents and I decided that, even though it was inconvenient, we would all find somewhere else to go on those weekends, so the boys wouldn't have to move. This is a practiced method of some divorced families; it's called "nesting." The little birds stay in the nest and the parents fly in and out. Usually the grandparent birds don't also have to fly in and out, and even though I could tell myself that my parents discovered new cities and had adventures, this monthly ritual must have been enormously troubling for the grandparent birds, and galling. Greater challenges have been faced and greater hardships met by families across the ages, but my parents' weekend situation then did make me think that your job as a parent isn't ever done, not until you are dead.

Pregnant, generous Sasha from my girlfriends' road trip said I could come down to her apartment and sleep in the baby's room, which was all set and ready to go for his June arrival. Sasha and her husband, Michael, lived on a beautiful

ISABEL GILLIES

tree-lined street downtown, and the change of scenery and neighborhood was a tonic and lifesaver during those awkward weekends.

I would pack my bag with the bare minimum. If I needed anything pretty, I could borrow something of Sasha's (most of the clothes I had used to be hers anyway). I would wait with the boys for Josiah to come from the airport, then participate in a limited but pleasant transition time—the twenty-minute nuclear family. When I did leave, I would clutch the rail in the elevator and practice *ujjayi* breathing until the door opened into the lobby. By the time I got to the subway platform, I had transitioned; I no longer felt the sting of leaving them, and him, behind.

You would think that I would have set up a lot of dates during these weekends, but one has to be asked on a date, and you can't really plan for that to happen at all, much less exactly when your ex-husband will be coming in from Ohio. I don't remember one date from those weekends. What I do remember is washing my hair with Sasha's shampoo and eating Michael's tofu scrambles.

Gestation. It seemed fitting to spend these weekends with a pregnant person and her spouse. There is a quiet to developing something, anything. When you are developing an idea, you roll it around in your mind, think about it. There is a quiet to thinking. There is a quiet to pregnancy, too. Especially a first pregnancy. You listen for heartbeats and stop to feel kicking. Dream up names. Sebastian, Marco, Billy, Cyrus. You rest, sleep, and take your time.

Ever since I met Josiah, I had felt that I was somewhere

loud, like on a subway. Much of the noise was joyful. Clinking of toasting glasses, wedding songs, barking puppies, careers, moving trucks, screaming babies, laughing babies. Some of it was sad, like when Josiah told me he was leaving—our clamorous parting. But now that my time with Josiah was over, and Wallace, James, and I were in our cocoon, developing, there was a quiet again. And it was winter, a fitting season to spend some time with my friends who were also gestating.

Michael had created the tofu scramble to check off nutritional boxes for Sasha and the unborn child. The scramble was tofu, broccoli, spinach, peppers, onions, and herbs all tumbled together in a wok with sesame oil and maybe a little soy sauce. Michael chopped and peeled; he toasted bagels in the kitchen, then brought the big steaming bowls out to the two of us, where we sat at their farmhouse table waiting like schoolchildren. The entire morning was taken up by piling the scramble onto the bagels, talking, and drinking tea and orange juice.

The three of us spent half the day trying to figure it all out. What went wrong? Could I have predicted it? Could I have prevented it? What was she like? Would it last? How were the boys going to cope? What were we going to name that baby? How would Sasha's and Michael's lives change because of him? Would they be able to make room for the little fellow? Would they be good parents? Would I ever meet someone? Would that person be a friend of theirs? Did I want to meet someone? Was I scared? Were they? What if they dropped the baby? What if something went wrong? What if something went right?

We would cover all the bases without getting dressed. Later

in the day, I might go to the movies or dinner with another friend, but mostly I would just stay in their little West Village apartment and think about everything. What is the lesson here? It was hard not to check in on the boys and Josiah. It was hard letting go of my family, though I believe you should really leave the other parent alone during their time with the children.

You want to micromanage, but it's better if you don't. What feels good for you and what is good for the children are different. That is a hard pill to swallow. You have to be strict with yourself. It's easy and very explainable to use something like health as an excuse. "I just wanted to make sure you knew we had a thermometer. I thought maybe they were coming down with something." It's hard not to try to control something you really do have some business controlling, but shouldn't be controlling at that time. It's hard to trust. But you've got to, pretty much anyone is capable of getting a thermometer, and it's good for the kids to learn that there are a variety of ways to do things, that both Mom and Dad can put on the Band-Aid. That they can love different people for different reasons. This last one is especially important with stepparents. It's challenging for kids to feel good about loving both the dad and the stepdad, the mom and the stepmom. There are loyalty issues and mixed messages from adults. The number and variety of adults who sometimes come into a kid's life because of a divorce is a beast. Kids need to learn flexibility and tolerance to endure their future of living in many different homes with different parents. They need to believe that they are okay with all of their parents, even the evil stepmonster. It was better that they started sooner rather than later getting familiar with that, and feeling good about it.

Although I got a large amount of thinking done, those weekends were quick. Before I knew it, Sunday afternoon would come and I would take the C subway train back home to help the kids say good-bye. Even before the divorce, I'd hated Sundays (and hated saying good-bye). To me Sundays are blue days, too long and with a sadness to them, even in the happiest of times. And the transition from the dad weekend back to the mom week is hard. Everyone is left with a thousand-piece puzzle of complicated feelings. My Sunday evenings on those weekends were spent on the floor with the kids, on the phone with Josiah (from the airport), at the table with my parents, back on the phone with a friend, talking it all out, picking through the pieces to a puzzle whose whole image I was not yet able to see. (And even now, with a much clearer picture of where the pieces go, I still spend those Sundays doing the puzzle.)

chapter 23

You know when something sticks with you? In my twenties I read Rainer Maria Rilke's *Letters to a Young Poet*. If you have not read that book, go out and get it now and read it. It's a collection of letters from the poet Rilke to a younger poet. There are a bunch of letters in the book, and every one of them is a gem. In letter four, the young poet must have been confused about something; perhaps he found himself in a situation where he just didn't know what to do. Rilke's advice was to "love the questions themselves." Love the questions.

Rilke went on to say, "And the point is, to live everything, live the questions now. Perhaps then, someday far in the future, you will gradually, without even noticing it, live your way to the answer."

Live your way to the answer. From the moment I read that I thought it was the smartest thought anyone had ever had. But it's a tough prescription, because most of us want the answers now. It's hard to love the scary questions. What happens if I go broke? Will I ever love again? Will my children be okay?

What Rilke is saying is to live. Live, live, live.

Another wise thought, which my father laid on me throughout my life, was to ask other people how they live. Ask people what they do and how they do it. It will help you. You can also read biographies to get answers, but that takes more time, years maybe, than simply asking for advice.

If you are a woman in crisis, there is no better place to seek advice than *women*. Women are like full, ripe orchards of apple and peach trees. Women are museum guides telling you the hidden meanings. Women are ponds. They look placid and simple, but my God, they teem with life and information an inch below the surface. There are incredible microcosms of information in those waters; there are hundreds of species of information. Women are encyclopedias, they are oracles, they are entire self-help sections of Barnes & Noble. Women! If you have a question or need advice, gather some women together. They will help you.

I was feeling like I had to kiss someone. I didn't want to kiss because I felt like kissing. No. I was worried about kissing. There wasn't anyone around to kiss (and I am not even remotely talking about sex; sex was not on my mind). But someone might show up. Then, out of nowhere, I could be faced with a kiss, and worry about that was freaking me out. I *love* kissing! Who doesn't? I can think of eight great kisses from the movies and from my life right this instant:

- The kiss that Eric Stoltz gives Mary Stuart Masterson in the movie *Some Kind of Wonderful*.
- The first big kiss I ever got, on my friend's Kermit bunk bed (from a guy named Oscar; yes, we were a

group of friends who called ourselves the Sesame Street gang).

- The kiss Judd Nelson gives Molly Ringwald in the movie *The Breakfast Club*. (Sorry, but those John Hughes kids were good at kissing.)
- My sophomore year at NYU, under that big arch in Washington Square Park, in the rain.
- At age twenty-four, at the train station in Bologna with Raphael, the Italian student who protested wars on the cobblestone streets and wore a white jean jacket.
- Big kiss with a friend (whom I never kissed again) after watching *The Godfather*. Something about that movie—
- The first kiss I had after the divorce.
- The second kiss (and most important of my life) I had after the divorce.

Okay, back to the women. A few weeks after I got back from the courthouse in Elyria, I was out to dinner in the city with three good friends I know well because our families have always spent summers on the same island in Maine. Amanda had just moved to New York with her daughter and husband. They had lived in New Orleans, and although it probably felt like leaving a child behind, they made the decision after Hurricane Katrina to start all over in the Big Apple. Amanda, among other things, is the kind of person who will take your hand while you say something sad (a gesture I find touching); she has been married for almost twenty years. The next was

Marina who had given me the black dress. Marina, besides being ethereal looking, like something out of a John Singer Sargent painting, is intelligent, and she always shows up. I had gone to her wedding almost ten years before. And the third was Lois. This was her night. Lois is a marvelous actress who got to make movies in the seventies when, let's be honest, the best movies were made. (I'm going to use my film-student-who-worked-for-a-year-at-a-snobby-underground-video-store credential to back up my last statement.) I had always admired Lois from her role as the glamorous Diane-Sawyer-with-a-twist role in *Broadcast News* (one of the movies I would want to have with me if I were stranded on a desert island), but she was also in *The Great Gatsby* and had been a "Bond girl." She is an artist, remarkably generous, sage, and has this soft and elegant Texan accent infused into her deep, voluptuous voice. Getting advice from a voice like that is like getting advice from James Earl Jones; you just take it and do it, plus there are brains and experience backing it up. She finally gave in to marriage in her fifties when a dashing and powerful tycoon asked her so many times she caved. As if calling the meeting to order, she signaled to the waiter for a pitcher of margaritas and numerous tasty, cheesy, savory little hot things to go with them. She kept everything coming without any of the rest of us thinking about it.

"I'm just so freaked out about kissing," I said, and took a swig of my frothy drink. This question was the real reason I went out to dinner that night, but we talked about many subjects that surrounded the kissing issue—the challenge of starting anything new, the challenge of finding someone nice, the many imperfections of life. No one there, even if it was un-spoken, had had a perfect life. From the outside, it certainly looked as if they had perfect lives, but if you listened, there were traces of sorrow, loss, complication, and fear laced through the discussion. Nothing outright, just flickers of the eye or of a hand unconsciously resting on a heart, subtle gestures that told me I wasn't alone in living with some kind of flawed situation.

My situation was funny, too, as imperfections often are. Much of the humor came from thinking about jumping into bed with someone at my age. I'm not saying I was old, but I was a long way from the twenty-six-year-old who could take it all off and do everything on the floor with the lights on. I can offer this: Lighting and sheets are your friends for post-baby sex with someone you didn't have the babies with. And I will divulge something here that I hope will make you happy. I have since learned that even if you have had babies and you do have sex with someone you didn't make them with, eventually you can take it all off and do everything on the floor with the lights on.

As for the kissing, Lois told me this—and she told it like she was Martha Stewart advising on how to decoupage a break-fast tray, something difficult but ultimately something you will find useful—for my first kiss I was to kiss someone I *didn't* want to marry. Not even close. If I even had a shred of feeling that I might want to get serious with the person, that was *not* whom I was supposed to kiss first. Pick someone inappropriate, someone you wouldn't want to get serious with and who wouldn't want to get serious with you. Lois almost made it sound like I should just ask someone on the street to lay one on me. Just to get it over with. And that's pretty much what I did.

. . .

My best friend Bess was turning thirty-six. For her birthday, she and her husband, George, took a group to dinner at an Austrian restaurant downtown. You know how there are maybe four perfect evenings each spring? This was one of them. Bess's birthday evening had that magical air about it, that spring feeling of blossoms and of balmy, fresh air. And we were in the West Village, a neighborhood of small brownstones with ivy crawling all over them, of sweet cafés, charming hat shops, artists, bookstores; the neighborhood tripled the natural blissed-out feeling that one of the four perfect evenings in spring can give you.

I was seated next to Sam, one of George's friends from college. Sam is a very funny writer who works for PBS. He's nice-looking and he talked out of the side of his mouth. He seemed like a guy who'd be a carpenter in Vermont. If Sam were a fictional guy, he would live in Vermont and have gone to Middlebury. Maybe he was originally from a big city, but he had fallen in love with the beauty and friendliness of that part of the world. He had lots of foodie guy friends who were intelligent and knew how to make venison stew. Maybe they even hunted the deer themselves. He and his friends read a lot and participated in helpful ways in the community. That was what Sam felt like. And, like I said, he was funny, funny, funny.

The real Sam was single, lived in Brooklyn, had a room-mate and I don't believe had any ambition to suddenly have two children and a wife. During dinner (I ordered beautifully that night—a tiny beet salad, then a delicious Wiener schnitzel with extraordinary cloudlike spaetzle, hugged by strands of wispy caramelized onion running through all of it—and there was also lots of cold white wine being poured all over the place), Sam teased me about looking all dressed up (we had met once before and I guess I hadn't looked so hot), and he told a hilarious, self-deprecating story about a cat getting lost. I sensed everyone at the table was watching us like hawks. I would giggle at something he said, and six eyes would dart around saying, "Did you see that? He's killing her." It wasn't a setup; well, of course it was, but basically the intention was to give the single kids a good time. After toasts to Bess, sweets, and tea, the dinner ended and everyone filed out onto the side street to mill around and say good night. We were all holding on to Betty Boop checker sets that had been given as table presents. When the married couples started hopping in cabs, Sam said, "I'm going to walk."

"Okay, good night!" I said too loudly, and hopped into the cab with Bess and George.

We took off southbound down Greenwich Street.

"What are you *doing*, Rudy?" Bess and George almost yelled at me.

"What?" I blushed.

"Sam is walking away!"

"I know. I'm shy!"

"Oh, Izzle, it's a perfect night. You should get out and go get him," urged Bess.

Then I thought about Lois. Kiss someone you really don't

want to marry. Sam was great. It wasn't that I would never, ever, in a million years marry him. It was that it was extremely clear we were in such different life spaces it would be irresponsible for either of us to marry each other, or even date each other. Sam was what she meant. Kiss someone who is in a wholly different time of life from you so it's *only* about the kiss and nothing else. Don't confuse issues.

You see, I *was* growing up. Fifteen years before, I would have wanted to kiss the guy and marry him. I would definitely have confused the issues. My evolution might have taken a bit longer than one would have liked, but I wasn't confused now. Yes, I had to kiss someone, but I was going to be damn careful about whom I married. I could trust myself. I could even bet on myself. I wasn't going to make a mistake. It had taken a long time, five or six too-complicated relationships, broken hearts, children, but I was clear now. The energy of this realization made me brave and made me want to kiss Sam even more.

"Well, okay. Here's what I'm going to do." It was like we were in *High School Musical.* "If Sam is on the corner when we get to Eleventh Street, if he hasn't crossed the street yet, I'll get out. If he has, then it wasn't in the cards."

"Oh my God!" Bess was excited. (Kooky romantic scenes are so much more fun if they're not happening to you.)

And of course, as we pulled up to the light at Eleventh Street, there was Sam, smiling on the corner, about to cross. George looked at me like, "Okay, lady, go put your money where your mouth is." I smiled, clutched my checkers set, and leapt out of the car.

"Well, what on earth are you doing?" Sam said in a sexy (I forgot to tell you that he was from Texas), slow accent, amused.

"Bess and George were going the wrong way so—"

"Don't you all live on the Upper West Side?"

"Yeah, but I'm on CPW and they are on West End, so really unless you want to cross like seven avenues, then you really should take different cabs from the very start."

"Uh huh," he said. We walked up Eleventh Street holding on to our checkers sets as if they were schoolbooks.

"I'm just, let's see. Sixth Avenue goes north, so—" I was squinting at street signs like I was trying to figure it all out. The truth is, in my twenties, I had lived in that neighborhood for years.

"Uh huh," Sam said.

I stopped in front of a particularly charming brownstone under a light-pink, wildly blooming fruit tree, faced him directly, and spoke very fast. "Sam, here's the thing. I have two kids and a whole lot of baggage and you don't want to get into all of that. And I don't want to and can't really spend even one night in an apartment way down in Brooklyn, not that I don't like Brooklyn, I do, I lived there before I was married. But it's far away from where I live and I can't leave my kids and anyway— well, I haven't kissed anyone except my ex-husband in almost ten years, and—"

Sam dropped his checkers on the ground, took hold of my waist with one hand and the back of my neck with the other, and gave me a kiss right out of one of those John Hughes movies I love so much.

It was done. Sam had ripped the Band-Aid off.

"Wow. Thanks," I said.

"You are welcome, lady. Can I get you that cab now?" he said like Matthew McConaughey.

Sam hailed a cab on Sixth Avenue. I got in it, waved out of the back window, and flew uptown to my parents' apartment where my boys would be waiting for me even though they were sleeping. At Columbus Circle, the Kelly Clarkson song "Since U Been Gone" came on the radio. Recognizing the bass guitar right away, I asked the driver if he could turn it up really loud.

Do you know this song? It's a "moving on" anthem. Kelly Clarkson (I wish I could sing like her—oh, I really wish I were a mammoth rock star of any kind) lets this song rip. It's about a guy she loved, and it didn't work out, but now she is *so moving on*. On that glorious spring night, I felt like I was moving on, and this was the perfect song to soar up Sixth Avenue to while the wind rushed through the open taxi window.

chapter 24

The first bill I got for West Side Montessori was in the thousands. I had been expecting this and had prepared for it. I was working. I had sold the house. Josiah's parents were helping some. But even with a generous portion of the tuition paid for by the school and even with all the preparation put in place to pay my share, the number set something off in me that dissolved any assurance my attempts at organization had given me. I had money panic. Money panic is massive, and I am convinced that it feels similar whether you have ten million dollars or ten.

How am I going to do this? I felt an involuntary deep breath happen, I felt my mouth turn down and the burn of tears on my eyes. Goddamn it, don't cry. (I cry so much, and so does my mother. I asked her about it once. "Mum, did your mother cry? Did Granny Carter? 'Cause what is the deal with how much you and I cry?" My mother said, "You know, they didn't. They didn't really cry. They were good emotional people, but they didn't cry like we do." It must be that Mum and I are crying for everyone in our family before us.)

I bit my lip and looked up at the ceiling, shook my hands out. *You can do this, Isabel. Don't lose it.*

I didn't know where the kids were. Watching TV? I admit that I did put them in front of the TV while doing things such as opening bills, taking a shower, or returning a phone call. I felt shy about doing it in front of my father. I don't think he views TV and kids as a very good mix. Whenever I put them in front of the boob tube, as he calls it, he would subtly get up from whatever he was doing and go sit with them, kind of scooping them closer to him and propping them out of that television slump. "Wallace, why do you think that crazy cat climbed all the way up there? James, look at all those colors, which ones do you like?"

Anyway, they were probably safely glued to the television, and my mother was working in her room ten feet away. I felt like I was eleven years old with homework that was too hard for me. As much as I wanted to still my anxiety by myself, I needed help.

"Mumma," I chirped outside her door that was almost always left open.

"Lool? Is that you?" I pushed open the door to see her at her desk. She turned, taking off her reading glasses.

"Loolie, what's the matter, my sweetheart?"

I came in, sat on the end of her bed, hunched over, and started weeping. I hadn't cried to my mother since I'd arrived from Ohio. I had cried in front of her, but not to her.

"I am so scared. I am so terrified I won't be able to do this. It's all so much. They need so much of everything, and I don't know if I can give it to them. I'm going to screw it up. I just don't think, well, what if I can't do it?"

"Oh, my baby." She sat beside me, wrapping her arm around my crumpled self. "Don't you worry. Look at you. Look at what you have done. It will work out. It just will. You are doing a marvelous job, and we're not going anywhere, Lool."

She didn't mean they would pay for school or make it so the kids weren't sad, or even that they wouldn't eventually go somewhere far away from me and the boys. She just meant I wasn't alone. She rocked me side to side ever so slightly on her pretty blue-and-white bed. Nobody ever makes me feel as good as she does.

I heard what she said, and that moment with her was enough to help me recover for the evening and take some little steps forward—make dinner for the boys, fold the clothes left on the floor, call my manager to check on auditions, pluck an eyebrow, play a round of Go Fish, make a to-do list, return an e-mail, balance my checkbook, send a thank-you note. I still felt something that has stayed with me from being divorced, though, and that is that I was responsible for the kids. I was. No amount of my ex-husband, or parents, or anyone else telling me that they were there, too, ever eased my real belief that it was me or nothing.

Even though I did figure out how to pay for the kids' preschool (now they are in public school), the feeling of it's-me-or-nothing has never gone away. That is where I was wounded by the divorce, and where there is still a bloody hole.

chapter 25

"Dolla? Are we ready?" That is my mother asking my father if it's time to go into the kitchen and do every-man-woman-leftover out-of-the-fridge-lunch on a Saturday afternoon.

"Cheers, Yox!" That is my father toasting my mother every night when they have drinks before dinner.

"Yanchel [pronounced: Yayn-chal], do you want to do messages?" That is my father asking my mother if she wants to listen to the voice mail, together, with yellow pads.

"Huh-*huh*." That is the noise my parents make as if to say, See you later.

You want to get that marriage thing right. The relationship, God willing, precedes and outlasts child rearing. And you *choose* it. You have control of who you get.

Maybe a good marriage is just a feeling that lives between two people. I always knew my parents had something good because I could see it from the backseat of our Jeep. We kids would all sit in the backseat—sometimes there were two of us, sometimes four, depending on whether or not my half-brothers were with us. If they were there, that would place my brother Andrew and me in the middle of the backseat. The teenagers folded themselves into the car next to either window, flanking Andrew and me. The big boys had a comforting musty smell and tremendous knees that came up like mountains on either side of us little ones. From my vantage point, I looked between my parents in the front seat. My father always drove. If a particularly good song came on the radio—I'm thinking Fleetwood Mac—my parents would join hands, hold their locked hands up, and gently rock their arms back and forth to the beat of the music. Swing, beat, swing, beat; dance driving. They didn't look at each other. They just rocked back and forth and quietly sang, "Ooooh, don'tcha look baaack," to the AM/FM radio in the dashboard.

In my thinking about marriage and what I was made of, I looked back a few generations. My maternal grandparents, Mimi and Phil, never divorced, but I had heard hushed rumblings of infidelity. I also heard about how much they adored each other. My grandmother wore her hair in two long braids that fell over her shoulders. I can remember watching the two of them walk down in the twilight to their little house on an island on the Saint Lawrence River called Whisky. There were huge, domed rocks that came out of the ground, interrupting the lawn like giant turtle shells. Because the rocks were so big, you could walk across them. I can see in my mind's eye my grandfather in his Guatemalan red-striped jacket taking hold of my grandmother's delicate hand so she didn't lose her footing in her loose-fitting sandals. One of their Labs would always be with them, trotting just ahead, scaring away snakes. I can still hear them calling out lovingly to the dog, one after the other, as if they were in a conversation together. My grandmother drew and painted birds; my grandfather took photographs of birds. They traveled around the country in a van seeking out warblers and falcons. I always thought their mutual love of birds was pretty good.

I know that my maternal great-grandparents had a wonderful marriage and that my great-grandfather had a mistress. They were expatriates living in Paris because my great-grandfather headed up an American bank there. When I was in my early twenties and starting to talk about what it might be like to get married and beginning to consider the different relationships in my family, my mother told me, among many other observations and pieces of ancestral information, that her grandfather had a mistress; let's call her Ms. X. I am almost positive that there were not two people on earth that my mother loved, admired, looked up to, and emulated (in lots of ways, but not the extramarital affair way) more than her grandparents. She simply told me about what she remembered to guide me; it was more like a history lesson than a critique.

Ms. X used to give my mother beautiful nightgowns when she was a child. What? An elegant woman who was my grandfather's mistress was allowed to give the granddaughter nightgowns? What made my formidable granny tolerate it? All I can think was that it was a different time, and they were in France. Apparently, when Granny Carter's husband was on his deathbed (he died quite young, in his sixties) and everyone was gathered around in the hospital room, at some point Granny said to the group in French, "Okay, please leave the room so Ms. X can say farewell to Granpère."

The family filed out, and Ms. X entered.

Once our marriage had started to crumble and it was pretty much established that Josiah was in love with Sylvia, in hopes of saving the marriage there was a part of me that wanted to turn my head and let the affair happen. In fleeting, intellectualized, or confused, desperate but sort of sane moments, I wanted to allow their relationship to take its course if it would keep my family together. In some ways, who cares? So someone falls in love or wants to have sex with another person? We are all animals. Maybe Granny-in-France had it right. Instead of calling her husband out, intimidating him with drama, she let it happen. And Granny Carter was no shrinking violet. She was a strong, intellectual lady, who maybe knew how to play a certain game, or was more tolerant of human transgression than her great-granddaughter. She got to keep her powerful, handsome husband and father of her children who adored her. Her granddaughter might have slept for a few nights in lovely nightgowns given to her by the other woman, but nobody ever left my great-grandmother. I could see myself as being too jealous. Maybe Granny was more secure than I was. Maybe her life was unbearably painful. I don't know. It was Edwardian.

And what about this way of looking at what happened to my marriage: My husband left me for another woman, but we were all crammed into the same minuscule town together. I walked in on an intimate moment (not sexual, but intimate) between the two of them because my office was so close to theirs. What if we had lived in New York? What if he had taught at Columbia and I at NYU, which are five miles away from each other? I would have never seen and felt the intimacy between them, never would have confronted it. In a way, I might have defined their relationship as a relationship. I did. I asked if they were in love. I said, "Swear on the children that you are not in love with Sylvia!" I caused the scene. Maybe if I had never seen it, it would have just gone away. They were both married. Were they really going to cause all that ruckus themselves? We will never know, but maybe not. Maybe they would have just dreamed about each other, longed for each other, fantasized, but never acted. Maybe I made them do it— gave them the big idea. It makes me ponder something even more terrifying. What if when I saw them and sensed that undeniable feeling between them, instead of just letting it be, leaving it alone, I impulsively called them out in a big way and I did it because *I was unhappy* and saw a way out? I didn't want to do what my great-grandmother did and turn my head. It's not in my personality to turn my head. I'm a confronter, but what did I create when I named how they felt, maybe for only one moment, straight on and made a big deal about it? I made it real for all of us and quite possibly carved out my destiny.

I hate that thought, because at the time I would have never said I was unhappy. I thought our life was good. I bet everything on it.

I don't have a big enough telescope to see with undeniable clarity why something works and why it doesn't when it comes to matters of the heart between two people. So much of it is like a shooting star; you can see the trail for only so long until it disappears. And a monstrous portion of why a marriage works is about the individual, what happens inside a person day to day—and how can anyone know what that is or make any sense out of what happens inside another person? All I could do was let the information I had about myself and parts of my family sit in me and brew.

But the wanderings into the past and navel-gazing might have gotten me somewhere, because in the early spring, I did have a revelation about what kind of relationship I wanted next.

. . .

The day had been surprisingly warm for early spring, and as evening drew near, I asked my father if the boys and I could join him when he took Plover out for a walk. The air was gray and soft.

It was nice being with my father. I didn't feel upended when I was around him. I didn't feel that my life was a mess or that I had screwed up. We frequently talked about the predicament I was in, but he was never judgmental about it or worried. He believed in me. That had been true all my life. My teacher once commented that during a parent-teacher conference, while my mother sat down immediately to get down to the business of what was wrong (I was dyslexic), my father strolled around the room looking at the student art on the walls until he got to mine. With delight in his voice he declared, "This one must be Isabel's!"

That evening in early spring, there were not many people

in the park. It would be dark within the hour, but there was no mistaking that the stark light of winter was receding and spring, with its longer, easier light, was preparing to emerge. Dad had been divorced, too. He had had two little boys at the time his first marriage ended. He knew from experience what the big change in my life was like, and at the time I first came back to New York from Ohio, Dad was my only friend in the world who knew from experience what I was going through.

The Great Lawn, which is exactly that, a great oval-shaped lawn on the west side of the park, looked like the English countryside of your dreams that evening, and it was empty. I had walked around that oval my entire life. On its west side looms the Beresford, with its famous terraces and towers, and on the east is the Metropolitan Museum of Art, filled with tapestries from Henry VIII's court and an ancient temple from Egypt. In the seventies when New York was broke, disorganized, and crime-ridden, the oval was a dust bowl, which I played in and around. In the eighties, I hung out on it with my girlfriends, listening to Grateful Dead bootlegs on our boom boxes, smoking cigarettes, and doing homework. By the time Wallace was a newborn in 2001, thanks to generous New Yorkers and a large-scale restoration project by the Central Park Conservancy, the Great Lawn had been reborn. It was a glorious place to nurse a baby—sitting under the blooming cherry trees with other young mothers, eating turkey sandwiches, and chatting about tummy time and whether or not to go back to work.

The oval is the center of Central Park, the very heart of it.

Dad handed Plover's leash to me and said, "Come on, boys! Let's run across the whole oval, straight to the other side, then we can run back!"

With that, the three of them, Dad so tall in the middle, took off running, heads back, arms beating up and down. What a sight. My two little boys running alongside their up-for-it-all grandfather, just running. I thought, sitting on the sidelines, that it was deeply good that they knew each other. I thought that if I were still in Ohio, they wouldn't be running with him across that expanse of green with New York City behind them. *What if they never knew him?* I almost thanked God for my divorce at that moment. The boys looked relaxed and free and loved.

Dad. He taught me not to ignore the bigger picture, he taught me how to kill a fly (hold your hands directly above the fly and then clap), and he taught me at that moment that if someone came along who would run across lawns with my boys, I should choose that person.

chapter 26

I didn't want Sylvia to see the children, but I knew my re-
fusal to be realistic would frustrate Josiah so much that it
might compromise the quality of time he spent with the boys,
just because, of course, he would prefer to see his children
along with the woman he loved. Also, refusing to let what-
will-be be is petulant and controlling. I knew that, so I loos-
ened my grip on the joystick and said Sylvia could be with
Josiah on the next visit to New York. Wallace and James and
Josiah and Sylvia would go to the zoo, buy ice cream cones, et
cetera. Ugh. Life was moving right along.

The boys came home from that first "with Sylvia" weekend
with two amusing little wooden bird whistles. Instead of shrill,
vexing noises, the whistles sang like a real American Gold-
finch outside your bedroom window. The boys marched into
the apartment clutching them and happily chirping away. As
much as I wanted to *hate* those gorgeous little whistles, I would
have had to have been blind not to notice that the boys loved
them. It's hard to ignore joy—*even though I didn't have a boyfriend yet, or even a crush on anyone!*

I have felt on both sides what it is to be judged and to judge when it comes to stepparenting, and let me tell you, both sides are a bummer. I have questioned, from my mommy-from-afar perch, the other parent's choice of TV show, jacket weight, how high in the tree the kids can climb, and ice cream flavor. (Well, one time she, with every good intention, gave one of them high-octane coffee ice cream after dinner; come on! The kid didn't fall asleep till eleven. Now, it was not war in Iraq, but I did make it known that such an ice cream choice was a JV move.) A sizable chunk of my own parenting has also been held up to the I-think-you-do-that-wrong light. It's unpleasant on either end. All anyone can possibly do with kids is get it close-to-right, and, I think, the sooner everyone can be cool with close-to-right, the happier everyone will be.

And sometimes the noncustodial parent brings something to the table that you can't provide and you want your children to have. In my case, it was bird whistles and French. I can't speak French, Sylvia can, and I want my kids to speak French. And, well, I think she is a lot calmer than I am.

It turns out that being civilized is more fun than one might imagine. How cool and happy do Bruce, Demi, and Ashton look? I don't mind using celebrities as examples, by the way. People have been looking to their kings and queens as examples of how to live life for centuries, and as far as I can see, movie stars are what we have now. As someone pointed out to me recently, we are all struggling; you take inspiration and instruction where you can get it.

If it feels uncomfortable, try to find the bird whistles. It turns out Sylvia is kind of great, especially with the boys. She might actually teach them French, she bakes cakes from scratch with James (for hours), and she understands that Wallace is magical. She's doing a good job, and I saw it first through the whistles.

chapter 27

Easter landed on March 27 that year. A tad early. The week before, I had felt myself inspired by everything from the emerging shoots of the daffodil leaves coming up in the park to *Martha Stewart Living* and *Gourmet* covers at the magazine stand on Broadway. It was the first holiday that we would have in the apartment, besides that past Christmas, which in my mind stands out like a chapter of *Alice in Wonderland* it was so weird, and my thirty-sixth birthday in February, when we were all sick, freezing, and I had happened to get a particularly bad haircut (bangs). During the little birthday party my parents and I had with the boys, my mother made a disapproving face (she has never liked bangs), which I took too personally. We all despaired.

By Easter, the new season was giving me a boost. I now wanted traditional meals that were meaningful and jolly, and new photographs that I could later glue into albums. I even wanted to cook.

The boys and I sat on the cork floor of the kitchen and

dipped dripping yellow and blue eggs into brightly colored bowls of Paas dye all afternoon. Their stained fingers still smelled of the vinegar when I sang them to sleep that evening.

"Where should we hide the eggs?" I asked my parents later that night. "In the apartment?" I knew there were five thousand acres of green grass across the street in Central Park, but needed encouragement.

"In the park!" my father said as if I were a fool.

"Oh, yeah, but—"

"We'll hide them in the morning and then call you up here. I'll take my cell phone," said my mother proudly. (My mother has a cell phone, but she still turns the entire thing off after she is through making a call.) "Then you and the boys will come down and they can find them in the Pinetum next to the oval. They'll have a ball!"

"I'll make a map tonight," my father said quite seriously as he cleared his and my mother's plates into the kitchen. "You can say that the Easter Bunny left it for them during the night so they would know where to go in the park. I'll do it after a little ice cream and chocolate sauce." Now that dinner was over, my mother rested her elbows on the table and took a sip of her wine. "It will be fun, Loola, what should we have? I didn't think to get a ham."

Planning meals, hatching plans, dog underfoot, boys asleep in bed. Family. As suddenly as crocuses, my broken little life didn't feel broken; it felt like a family.

Charles Ingalls, or Pa, in the TV version of *Little House on the Prairie*, always teared up when he had been through something tough—a flood, a blizzard, a fire, or typhoid—then found himself sitting at the farmhouse table surrounded by his family. They all would be well aware that they had almost lost something valuable. Typically, there would be a silent, knowing pause of being grateful, and then Carrie, the baby, would break the tension with an off-the-wall comment or sweet remark that would make everyone laugh. The last shot would be of Charles looking at Caroline (Ma) with a tear in his eye, signifying, "It's all right, we are together."

For me, that is what I had been gunning for most of my life: the table, Ma and Pa, family. Having things go wrong but then ending up all together—that's the life I wanted.

I was sure that when my marriage failed I had lost that opportunity. I screwed it up, or he did, or we both did, but my chance at family was gone. I came home a failure to my own dream. Even though right there, under my nose, were a Ma and a Pa and a table and even tears in eyes. Even at my lowest moment, I had a family.

The boys awoke to a bird's-eye-view map drawn by the Easter Bunny himself on yellow legal-pad paper. It had our building with an "X" on it saying YOU ARE HERE. And then little dash marks down Central Park West, taking a left on Eighty-sixth Street, through the entrance of the park (indicated by trees drawn in brown and green markers), down the path, and over the bridle path (indicated by a better-than-stick-figure horse and rider), and ending in THE PINETUM right before the Great Lawn. START!

Wallace and James were delighted by the map and followed it in their white-and-blue pullovers like Lewis and Clark all the way to where my parents stood, beaming, holding the dog.

I wore a long purple sweater coat that, again, was a Sasha hand-me-down. It felt warm and was the right color to be in on Easter morning. My mother and I had decided to get really good sliced ham from the deli and have sandwiches. In a few years, I would be pureeing asparagus and trying to roast entire hams, but even though spring had our noses back in our cookbooks, we didn't push it. I should have gone to church. I think my mother even offered to watch the boys if I wanted to. I love the Easter service. It is joyful and full of rebirth. Lilies are everywhere and the most beautiful hymn in the world is sung on Easter, "Christ Is Risen! Hallelujah!"

When I sing the "Hallelujah" part, my heart swells so fully, it is like pure love. Pure love without a person attached. There is a lot of that in life, and not just in religious songs. If you can get that feeling out of swimming in a river, hearing your favorite new song on the radio, the smell of onions frying on a gyro cart on the corner, or anything else, grab it. Sometimes I even get a kick out of writing the number "5."

Even though I didn't sing the Hallelujah song, I did feel love as I watched my mother give James, whose basket seemed very large dragging behind the still impossibly young him, a hint about the pink egg next to the tree.

●　●　●

It took from October 6 to mid-December for my intact marriage to fall apart and from January to the very last day of April until I divorced my ex-husband and I met Peter. Seven months. It was a year after I met Peter that he proposed and I accepted marriage. One year.

I'm not sure I have ever said that sentence out loud because it sounds outlandish. It was quite something to write it. It just sounds so wrong. One marriage ends and you turn on a dime and start another one? Stranger things have happened, but still, writing down the time frame in which I changed gears spins my head.

But why? Most animals mate almost every six months with someone new. People fall in love within their marriages. Teenagers fall in love and it lasts for eighty years. Some people marry four times. Woody Allen fell in love with and married his stepdaughter. Henry VIII killed his wives when he wanted to marry someone else. Some men in Utah live with five or more wives. People whose spouses died in 9/11 fell in love with their grief counselors, who then left their spouses to marry their new beloveds. Many people are in love for a lifetime and never marry. Many marry someone they don't love. People divorce, marry someone else, divorce that person, and then remarry their ex-spouse. The mystery of human couplings is a big and unsolvable one. I would love it if everyone including myself just met someone, fell in love, got married, had babies, grew old, and died within minutes of that first spouse, but it just doesn't seem to happen that way.

So I'm not going to feel shy about the fact that I really did meet the love of my life months after my first marriage ended. That's the way it happened. Maybe it was because, miraculously, I was ready. Maybe my first marriage, even though it had its problems, wasn't that bad and I actually learned from the experience, like when someone wipes out really badly in their first Olympics but four years later is standing on the podium.

Sometimes, you don't even need to be totally ready. What is that, anyway? Are you ever ready 100 percent to jump off a dock into cold water or start a new job or move? Finding love might be more about being willing than ready.

And willing I was.

chapter 28

Friday, April 28, I was invited by friends to dinner at their apartment on the East Side. My parents volunteered to babysit, again. I chose a turquoise-blue dress that tied in the back, showing my waist, and rubbed new (if there is any time to change one's fragrance, it is the spring after you are divorced) orange blossom perfume into my wrists.

All dressed up, I kissed my boys on their damp, combed heads. I timed my departure to the start of a before-bed video. Anyone leaving was upsetting to them, especially me. I could see the worry and skepticism when their eyes briefly left the screen to mark that I would be going in the next minute or two. I remember from my own childhood the dread I felt when I suddenly smelled perfume and heard the clicking of heels on the hardwood floor. My parents, sensing my last-minute hesitation, enthusiastically urged me to go.

"We'll be fine. Have fun. You look nice."

I headed out into the night.

As the taxi turned right onto Park Avenue, I dabbed a little more shine on my lips and checked my hair in the reflection of the Plexiglas barrier between the driver and me. The couple having the dinner were friends, but not good enough friends to have me over just because. There had to be a reason. Owen was a banker. There was probably a guy in his office who had recently gone through a brutal divorce and who had two kids he picked up every morning at his ex-wife's apartment and walked three blocks to their school. He would be a perfect match for their friend from Maine who had just gotten back from Ohio. *Everyone was surprised to hear about the breakup, but it's lovely she's back in New York. She's living with her parents on the West Side. She has two kids.*

I asked the driver to drop me off on Lexington Avenue so I could find a deli and get flowers. I picked lilacs, which had only that week begun showing up around town. Who wouldn't like a girl who showed up with lilacs?

Elaine, the beautiful, really sort of perfect-looking, hostess, glided down the stairs from her bedroom, smiled, welcomed me, smelled the flowers with great appreciation, and handed them to Owen, her well-turned-out husband, who beamed, and as he asked what I would like to drink, he handed the flowers off to someone in the kitchen.

The living room was plumped, candles glowed, and little round toasts with bubbling goat cheese awaited eating on the coffee table. It was all so pretty and well planned, and, sweetly, Elaine and Owen had invited six friends, all couples, whom I knew well from Maine. There were nine of us, and that was it. That's the crazy thing—you are so aware of how single you are and what an effort it is to leave those kids, and so on and so on, that you just assume everyone else is hyper-focused on your singleness, too, and you in a rather self-centered way think that if they ask you somewhere it's because they have got your husband waiting there for you, or why would they have you cross town? You never think that people would want to include you just because it's nice to be included, until you are there and you realize that the entire world isn't as aware of your marital status as you are. I can't lie and say I wasn't disappointed that Prince Charming wasn't seated next to me at dinner. I had worn the prettiest dress I had and tweezed my eyebrows, and these efforts turned out to be for the benefit of old friends who wouldn't have cared if I wore blue jeans and a T-shirt.

Embarrassed about my expectation for the evening, I reminded myself as I passed through the Eighty-sixth Street transverse that I was fortunate to have such nice friends, friends who got me out of my parents' apartment for a jolly evening. And I was lucky to have a pretty dress to put on, and lucky to have New York City at night.

· · ·

The next day, Oscar, my oldest friend (really, there is a picture of our mothers together with great big tummies filled up by us), invited the boys and me to a gathering of pals and their kids in the Great Lawn Oval in Central Park. Having a plan for Saturday was a relief; that it was a gorgeous, warm day was a bonus. (I cannot drive home enough how ghastly weekends are for the single parent. A friend of mine who is a single mother of two was telling me just the other day that she is fine during the week—busy, distracted by school, afterschool lessons, et cetera. But on the weekends she wants to kill herself.) We arrived right on time, and my boys quickly merged with the other scampering children, running and throwing Nerf balls around.

I flopped on a blanket with the girls and let out the breath I had been holding ever since I'd started getting the boys ready to leave the apartment.

"You look pretty," said my straightforward and bubbly friend Fran, the one who said maybe it wouldn't be the end of the world if I just let Josiah go.

"I'm slightly hungover," I said.

"Well, I love the shirt," she piped back.

"It's from a tiny little Tibetan place on a side street somewhere." I still lay on my back with my eyes closed.

"Huh. When did you get the boys' hair cut?" she said, because she was sitting up, looking forward, and keeping an eye on the mass of five-and-unders. (One mother is always keeping an eye.)

The chat went on until eventually I got up, feeling that my flop time had expired and it was time to run around like a good parent.

Now, I'm not really a Monkey in the Middle person, but I wasn't about to organize baseball or anything, so I started corralling kids. All the parents joined in like sheepdogs nudging the galloping herd here and there, trying to line them up and tell them about the game. Every small person there was between two and five years old, James being one of the littlest at almost two. I had some awareness that there was a guy around me, who, like a senior camp counselor, actually did get the game going, but mostly the scene was mayhem. I ended up standing on my knees, waving my arms around with the organizing guy—we were the monkeys—as balls flew over our heads. I do know that he said his name was Peter, because I have always liked the name.

Afterward, I returned, panting, to the blanket.

"You are better than I am. I hate playing Monkey in the Middle," said Fran. Fran has girls, and even though they are active, you would usually find one or two of them nestled next to her using their fine motor skills. Thus, Fran was still on the blanket.

"I do, too, but I gotta play something with them," I said. I was freaked about sports. Dads play baseball with their kids. I know not all of them do, and I know there are a zillion moms who are awesome at it, but in my life it was my dad who was out with my brother and me playing catch, not my mother. I was going to have to do all the sports stuff now, and it seemed exhausting and impossible to have to invent something as large as a sporting life for two growing boys if it didn't come naturally to you. I would much rather teach them how to separate an egg.

I sat there watching Oscar swing Wallace, his godson, around. I pondered the sports problem.

"Um, are you *not* noticing the very cute *single dad* who is here with us today?" said Fran, as if she had been wanting to say that for three hours.

I blushed. I suddenly felt like I had no clothes on. "What? Well, yeah, I mean, I think I just played Monkey in the Middle with him? I think he's Oscar's friend Peter."

"Yes! I think it's Peter. He's a friend of Oscar's!" She was beside herself and repeating me.

I shifted my attention, which, honest to God, had not been on Peter. He was pointing out an imaginary finish line to his daughter in the newly grown grass.

I think he saw me look at him, or everyone decided to take a break, because before I knew it, he was flopped down near the blanket I was on.

"Hey. You're Isabel Gillies, right?" he said with a big, big smile. Goodness, he had a big smile.

"Yeah," I said, amused.

"I can't believe I never made this connection, but I think I worked with your brother at *Forbes*. Is your brother named Andrew Gillies?"

"Yes!" I said. I love my brother.

"That's awesome. I can't believe I didn't make that connection," he said again, annoyed with himself, as if he had missed an answer on a crossword puzzle. "He's a good guy," he said.

One.

Two.

Three.

Four.

Five.

Six.

My brother *is* a good guy. There was something about the way Peter pointed it out that made me think *he* was a good guy.

We talked. I told him (using sign language, as I had with the pediatrician) that I had been divorced. I pointed down at my ring finger and then took my thumb, jerked it to the right (indicating the ring flying off), and made a noise with my mouth, like *zip!* He smiled, with a kind, sympathetic look in his eye, and said, "Me, too."

He suggested in a hard-to-read-if-it-was-flirtatious-or-not way that we get together to commiserate about being single parents, divorced, and so on. Hindsight screws this up because, if I'm being realistic, I'm sure there was an underlying flirtation, but when an encounter is unexpected and overrun by children and strollers and ice cream sandwiches, you are not thinking, "Hey hey hey, this guy is a dreamboat." It's more like, "Oh man, am I missing nap time?"

Our kids ran around us playing and kind of tackling each other like siblings. The three of them are exactly fourteen months apart. And even six years later, they still go in descending order, in height, from oldest to youngest, like those wooden Russian dolls.

Later, I went over to talk to Peter, ignoring that he was on his mobile. He shushed me gently with his finger to his lips and gave me a smile. That killed me. Even with the children and baby wipes and soccer balls flying around us, his sexy hush slayed me a little.

. . .

Even if I had fallen in love with Peter on the Great Lawn, a place that felt as familiar to me as a front lawn (or your lobby, if you're a New York City girl), going forward from that feeling would have seemed impossible if I'd stopped to think about it. How was I going to follow up and start to have a real crush on Peter or on anyone when I had those children and lived with my parents? But before the thought of any far future had a chance to cross my mind, I noticed that he had left his kid's fleece on the grass by my stroller.

I had already been a stepmother because Josiah had been married before and had a child from that marriage. If I'd learned anything from that experience (and I learned a lot of wonderful things from that little, now big, boy), it is that when you return a child back to his mother on Sunday night, you'd better not forget the Patagonia pullover.

Peter had told me that when he and the mother of his daughter, Antonia, had separated, he moved close by into a building on Eighty-fourth and Central Park West.

"The banana building?" I said to him.

"Uh, I don't know. It's on Eighty-fourth Street?"

"Don't you think those designs on the outside look like bananas?" I waited with eyebrows lifted, like, duh, of course they do.

"I never thought of it, but I guess you are right."

"Well, they do, and we all called it the banana building growing up."

"Who's we?"

"My brother and I and probably anyone else who lived on the Upper West Side."

(Teasing. Flirting. Immediately when you meet Peter, you get the sense he wants to be in the loop about everything. If he doesn't know about a person, place, or thing that comes up, he will find out about it as soon as he can. He's the most curious person I have ever met, and he retains a lot of information, like if someone says they are from Miami, he will say, "Oh, did you go to Palmetto High School?" He can do that almost anywhere in the country. So when I made the sweeping statement that *everyone* called it the banana building, I could tell that I had something he wanted: information. He's a reporter. I found it dead sexy.)

Anyway, I lived on Eighty-eighth and Central Park West, so I put Antonia's fleece in the back of my stroller and went home.

When I got there I immediately put drowsy James in bed to nap and Wallace in front of a video. On the way to my room, I saw the purple fleece folded in the basket at the bottom of the stroller, pulled it out, and took it to my room, where I put it on my desk and stared at it. How should I get it back? Of course, I would walk with the kids down to the banana building and drop it in Peter's lobby, but should I leave a note? Yes, a note. I always leave notes. How weird not to leave a note. But should it be on a yellow pad? Or should I use the card stock with ISABEL GILLIES in dark blue lithographed on it, which my mother had given me for Christmas when I'd had to change my name back? Yellow lined paper or note card? Note card or yellow lined paper?

I lay on my bed, looked out the window onto the rooftops going west, and got an awfully weird feeling in my tummy. Who was this guy?

Peter and I had met briefly twice before. The first time was so many years before that all I remember was having a conversation with him on a staircase at a party in New York about going to school with Oscar. Then I'd met him again in a playground in Central Park when I was eight months pregnant with James.

Josiah and I had been visiting New York from Cambridge, Massachusetts, where we were living. We had planned to meet Oscar, his wife Gill, and their two kids for the afternoon; it just so happened that Peter and his daughter were in the same playground. We'd all gathered in the sandbox. I remembered Peter sitting on the wooden ledge of the box and Antonia in the sand, playing two feet away from Wallace. I remembered sitting across from them, next to Josiah, my belly almost touching the cold, late-April sand, it was so large. I could almost remember the subject of the conversation we were having. But Peter only remembers Josiah! How does one not remember someone who is eight months pregnant and probably dominating the conversation? Maybe it was the Control Tower (the imaginary people in heaven who plan your life) specifically not calling Peter's attention to me because exactly two years later we would meet, fall in love, and a year after that become engaged to marry. Three and a half years after that day, we would be married. But how could we know that? At that time, we were both married to different people, living in different states, on different paths, not on each other's minds so much that Peter doesn't remember even seeing me or the watermelon that was my tummy.

That afternoon, Wallace, James, and I set out to deliver the forgotten fleece. I took both the yellow pad and the card stock and envelope. When we got to the lobby, I asked the boys which one I should pick to write a note on. They didn't care, or even understand what we were doing in a lobby other than ours. I almost asked the doorman which paper to use, but then I took a deep breath and chose the card stock. I had a feeling that this would be an important note.

Dear Peter and Antonia,

I think this is Antonia's (the princess pin gave it away). We found it after you left. Nice to see you today. I would love to get together, if you had any time, to talk about divorce, and all things.

Isabel, Wallace, and James

chapter 29

R eally? Peter? You know we called him Giggles at college. I love Peter! But I never thought of you guys together," Gillian said, sort of perplexed-sounding on the other end of the phone line. (Of course I had to call Oscar and Gillian to get the lowdown on him.)

"Why?" I said, intrigued.

"I don't know. You are so— tall."

"What? Gill, I was married to a giant and look what happened."

At that point she squealed excitedly. (I'm telling you, the thought of new love throws people into a tizzy.)

"I don't know, but I think he's kind of great. He said my brother was awesome." Suddenly, I felt shy.

"Oh, my God. This is going to make Oscar nuts!"

That was true. Peter and I made Oscar, who is so close to both of us and cares tremendously about people's feelings, totally nauseated with anxiety, worrying about whether or not we would make it. I don't think he relaxed until he and Gill were standing up for Peter and me on our wedding day.

• • •

Thinking about dating Peter still makes my heart race. First you have to understand the kind of person he is. If there is a bummer errand you have to run across town, in the rain, that might interfere with something fun for him, like a baseball game on TV, and it might involve people that he doesn't know, and it might take three hours, instead of giving you a pain in the neck about it, he will cheerfully say, "No problem, we can do it together." Peter will send you the poster of Fernando Torres, the hot Spanish footballer, because once you were obviously taken by him during a game you were watching on TV. He understands detailed and difficult law cases and private equity deals, but he also subscribes to *People*. He will eat anything and wouldn't complain if you made him an omelet and toast for dinner most nights, but there is something about him that inspires me to cook elaborately. He expects you to do your best, go to the gym, put a comb through your hair, but has many times said I looked pretty when I have glasses on, reading in bed before sleep. Peter is sexy and a great tennis player. He left the world of banking to follow his passion for journalism, even though many people around him thought he was nuts. He doesn't like dogs, one obvious, weird personality flaw, which I will excuse in light of the rest of him. He sends you books without any expectation that you will read them; he has a surprisingly good singing voice, and I know that because he can sing every word of most Billy Joel songs on the radio and does when they come on; and he despises losing anything, even his place in a book. Peter adores every member of his large and close family and would go to the end of the earth for any one of them. I don't think he ever got less than an A in school, but he isn't snobby about what anyone else got. He's not the best at admitting when he is wrong, but he would prefer never to fight at all. He's a great dancer and will happily dance with you in the living room. He is a workaholic, as is his father. Peter is a wonderful father. One can see it in the way he will reach back and grab his kid's foot while driving. His whole message to those who love him is: I'm here.

On our first outing, he took me to a restaurant on Eighty-eighth and Broadway called Aix. He talked on his mobile to a source on the Enron case for the three blocks it took us to get there, which I found totally sexy, even if I did sort of feel dorky walking alongside him, trying not to listen to his end of the conversation. He apologized in a charming, if-we-are-together-this-might-happen-a-lot way as we sat down at the table. "Oh, please. It's all so interesting. Enron. Wow. No, no, be on the phone as much as you need to, I'm fine," I said. (Reminder, it was the first date.) Then I said, "I'm starving."

And he said, "Oh, we're gonna eat."

That sentence alone is as good as it gets because of the way he spoke the words, like he was teeing us up for a good time, setting the tone for the whole night. In response, I ordered a steak with French fries and creamed spinach on the side, but then, when that first flush of ordering subsided, we talked as easily as best friends. We covered the end of our marriages, our kids, parents, our jobs, New York, the news. We kept agreeing and saying, "That's how I feel/think/see it." Fluid, engaged conversation. *What is happening?*

He kissed me that night on the corner, and then we never stopped kissing because it was so awesome (a Peter word). We still kiss all the time, and the kids moan and squeal, "Ohhhhh yuck! Grooooosssss. Stoppppp it!" then giggle their heads off. Antonia particularly has a beautiful little giggle, just like her dad.

• • •

Is this happening? I am so in love. He is funny and smart and kind and hot and—what in the world is he doing with me? I wasn't having a self-esteem crisis, I was actually mystified. What was he doing with me? I had these two little boys, one still in diapers, and he seemed to love them already. Why? Aren't other people's children other people's children? They are hard to love, especially when they whine or act weird or smell funny. But he laughed when my boys said crazy stuff, didn't wince at a spilled anything. He just seemed to dig them. I dug his kid, too, but I'm a girl and a mother; I'd assumed it was easier for women to gather up any kid who was in the vicinity, tend to them, and even love them right from the start. But remember my friend Dave, who pretended to be the gorilla, who was so kind to my boy at the birthday party? Maybe I had underestimated everyone.

I lived with my sweet and ever-present parents. Dating me was more like dating someone who was sixteen rather than thirty-six. If we wanted to kiss, it had to be on a street corner, and as romantic as that is—please—he was a successful, attractive man and I'm sure there were scores of single ladies with their own charming little East Village apartments and high-paying lawyering/publicist/designer, cutie-pie jobs with endless free evenings to rock my man's world without all the trouble of bedtimes and nightmares, unexpected, swollen sore throats (for everyone), motherly conversations about school districts, ERB scores, and potty training. My clothes were hand-me-downs, and everything was slightly baggy with my own overuse and divorce skinniness. I was far from an heiress, and I had a complicated trunk of baggage that would always be lying around any hallway where I lived.

The first time he came to see me with his daughter was at the West Side Montessori spring fair. I was manning the bake-sale table. It was clammy weather, weirdly hot and cold. I had a fanny pack on, I was wearing a purple T-shirt that made horrible sweat stains, and had one giraffe earring on (the school fair was jungle themed) with rhinestones for spots. My dad and the boys were at the fair, too, though I wasn't exactly sure where they'd gone, so at least I didn't look burdened down with children, but there was not a single glamorous thing about me at that moment. And there Peter was with his kid in tow. She was in a stroller, chowing on grilled corn. He strolled all the way over to West End Avenue to buy a brownie from me and flashed that enormous smile. I gave his daughter her brownie and saw my bake sale co-chair friend give me an ex-cited thumbs-up.

Every morning I woke up, and if for one second I could get away from the involuntary smiles, daydreamy, deep breathi-ness of all that love inside me, I had a choked-up feeling that maybe it would all end, he would disappear. One day while walking with James down Lexington Avenue in a Biblical-level rainstorm, the kind that laughs at any umbrella you might be lifting toward the heavens, I began to worry that Peter might be swept away by a flash flood. I wasn't worried about my two-year-old, who was hanging on to my hand for dear life as I hoisted him up onto Eighty-third Street, avoiding the category-four rapid that had formed around the sewer. What if the hard, driving rain didn't let up? It would collect and rush down Lex and down every avenue and street in Manhattan, and all that water, flowing like tributaries, would converge at the bottom of the island, pooling into One World Financial Center, rising to the tenth floor, the offices of the *Wall Street Journal*, and sweep Peter out a window into New York Harbor, never to be seen again. I thought of his funeral, and how nobody would understand who I was, or why I was crying as if I were a widow.

But my fears about floods sweeping us in different directions were unfounded, and our courtship continued, feeling very much to me like a Woody Allen movie. Most of the time we spent together was on the Upper West Side with our kids—in the park, museums, and pizza parlors—or just the two of us out for dinner and a movie. The image of the slightly neurotic, tall WASPy blonde, hand in hand with a stocky Jew carrying a paper and wearing a Yankees hat, with three little New Yorky rascal-mixed-marriage kids scampering alongside up and down Columbus Avenue fit beautifully into some idea (I am positive, thanks to the hundreds of times I have seen *Annie Hall*) I had about the way New York love should be: the All State burgers on Seventy-second Street, documentaries about Frank Gehry, ordering in Thai food on random Thursday nights in his bachelor pad. My parents happily watched over the kids so I could run four blocks down Central Park West to have dinner with Peter. We courted over moo shu from carry-out containers and went over his childhood growing up in Roslyn, New York, with his twin brother; how he would go into work with his dad sometimes and have Egg McMuffins on the way; and how his mother did everything right. Peter sang me his summer camp songs. We talked about my growing up in Manhattan, riding to middle school on the Eighty-sixth Street crosstown bus, what boarding school was like (I went to one for two grades), the 1990s rock scene in NYC that was the soundtrack for my college years. We confessed the fuck-ups we managed to get into in our twenties, mistakes we felt bad about, and our convictions about trying to avoid future mistakes. We kissed a lot and listened to Bruce Springsteen, sometimes with baseball on in the background (which I liked because it reminded me of my father), and then I would scamper back home by ten. In the year before we moved in together, we probably spent only seven nights all the way through until dawn in the same bed, but we spent many days and hours in the playgrounds of Central Park and the Museum of Natural History with our three young kids, ages four, three, and two. I had grown up running through those marble halls, darting into rooms to marvel at the size of ancient bones, and eventually, as my parents became exhausted, our family would retreat to the darkened, quiet underworld of the Hall of Ocean Life. My brother and I lay on the floor under the great Blue Whale that hung from the ceiling. We would splay ourselves out as if we were going to make snow angels and stare up and into the folds of the beast's pale belly while my parents watched from a distance somewhere in the blue light.

So many years later, I saw our three kids splayed out in the exact same way looking up at the same whale. It was like I was reliving the best parts of my childhood with this new band of five; and I hadn't planned on it, I didn't mean to, it was an accident. None of us were supposed to be there, but in the most uncanny way, from the very start, our union felt like something that had been carefully charted out.

On some weekends, we drove around the suburbs (just for the hell of it) all jammed into Peter's Jeep, drinking hot chocolate from Starbucks, pretending we were a family until, eventually, we were. We played a new Keith Urban album over and over, practically on a loop. The hit single from it was about the beginning of a new relationship. We held hands as Keith sang about leaps of faith, once-in-a-lifetime love, and the sun shining. I don't know if people thought our relationship was crazy or too fast or a bad idea. Someone must have raised an eyebrow at the speed, the intensity of the scene of five people playing house, but if they did they kept it from us. I am grateful for that. I didn't think what we were doing was crazy or too fast or a bad idea; but I knew that leaping into a family that didn't start out together was going to be difficult for everyone, and that the complexities would morph and change like shapes in a kaleidoscope for a long time—we would always have to be on our toes. But I thought what we were doing was brave, and Peter kept giving me evidence that we were a team.

•   •   •

When I think back on when I knew for certain that marrying Peter was the right thing to do, it's sort of like when my dad was running through the oval with the boys: There was a defining moment.

Eventually Erica was accepted to a good labor-doula program. Earlier in the year she had pointed out that the children and I were getting born again and we needed her help, but now that it seemed we were out of the canal, she was moving on to other people in transition.

I had taken a part-time job teaching acting at the New School for Social Research, so once again I went to Craigslist to find another Erica. Well, I guess the deal with Craigslist is it's hit or miss. Oh, this new gal was nice enough. She had the same hippy vibe as Erica but without that great big bubble of kindness, calm, and responsibility that Erica floated in. When Erica was with the children, the feeling was that she was there not for the job, but because the universe had informed her that our apartment was where she needed to be. This other girl looked the part, had the references, insisted she would be a Robin to my Batman, but when we started working together, something was wrong. I didn't want to leave the kids with her, but I *had to* because my parents had already gone away for the summer and I needed to go to work. I remember one time standing in the lobby thinking I should take the elevator right back upstairs, call the school to say I was sick, grab the boys, and excuse the new girl forever—but then all my students would be waiting, having prepared their work for a class that they had paid for—so I went to work, but it was horrible, like getting on a plane you think might crash. The kids were always fine, but she frightened me and, irrationally, I thought if I fired her she might get really mad and do something weird.

The first weekend after she started working with us, I went with Peter and the boys over to Fran's house for a playdate. It was the first time Peter had ever seen me stressed out. I remember I was pacing and he was leaning against Fran's stove eating a zucchini fritter she had just made.

"I don't know what it is! She argues with me in a gentle way so no one would be able to detect she was arguing, but she is. And I think she looks at the kids sideways. I feel so terrible because I just gave her the job and apparently she *really* needs the money if she is going to be able to go to Brazil with her boyfriend (something I heard about endlessly—where were the dream catchers and the alphabet days of the week?), and the worst part is, I'm scared to leave the boys with her. I'm scared of her." I sort of whispered the last part.

I was expecting that he would be sympathetic, but what came out of his mouth next floored me. "You gotta fire her right away. Want me to sit with you while you do it?"

Want me to sit with you while you do it?

The offer just hung in the air along with the amazing smell of frying zucchini. I didn't say anything because the feeling of that heavy burden of doing it alone—the burden that I had felt for so long, even before I came back to New York—being lifted almost made me cry.

After his work the following Monday, Peter came over to our apartment and sat with me while I told the new girl that it just wasn't working out.

It was the most romantic deed anyone has ever done for me.

chapter 30

When Peter and his daughter came over to my parents' apartment for a meal, one of the waiting chairs got pulled up to the little blue kitchen table that my mother had set up in the kitchen when we came back from Ohio. The waiting chair was placed on the longer side of the table, in between Wallace and James. Because the other side of the table was against the wall, three kids were all that could fit. They would sit and eat waffle tacos (waffles folded in half like a taco and filled up with oatmeal and fruit) and chat while Peter and I leaned against the counter, watching them, pouring milk or cleaning it up. It was always a sweet scene, but one time I looked over at Peter and his eyes were filled up with tears. It wasn't that he was overwhelmed with joy at the little family we had made, it was something different. We waited until the dishes were cleared and the kids were playing in the living room with my parents, and then I tentatively asked him what he was feeling.

"I just don't know what they all think about this," he said, and the tears welled again.

I gathered his strong body right up into my arms because I understood, in my core, what he meant. When Peter and I fell in love, our hearts were still swollen and tender from our marriages failing, resulting in the inescapable and painful reality that all of our children would be navigating a less than perfect world, a world where their parents didn't live in one home. Even in an ideal (if that word can be used), gentle, and intelligently handled family breakup, there is no getting around the fact that your babies will at the very least feel confusion. There are worse emotions that they must bear; but even just imagining a confused child, trying to consider this kind of life, can make you quake inside. How do you explain new siblings, households, and parents to children under the age of six? How do you know what their insides feel like? How did I know with any certainty when I watched Peter pushing James on the swing that James understood that he was safe and that the-guy-who-isn't-his-father would not let him fall? How can anyone know that what they are doing is absolutely right? Peter was feeling that heavy burden that I had felt so many times, the burden of getting it right for your children. As happy as we were and as good a plan as our new life seemed to be, we were parents first, and it wouldn't have been real if the difficulty didn't back up on us sometimes. But what we were doing was real, and, thank God, we were able to see it for what it was and hold on during the times when Keith Urban wasn't singing about the sun shining on a brand new day.

. . .

The restaurant P.J. Clarke's at Third Avenue and East Fifty-fifth Street is more than 130 years old, a two-story brick building among skyscrapers. I'm sure many real-estate bigwigs have wanted to tear it down, because a much taller building could be built on its valuable real estate, but the building has stood its ground so far, and still serves some of the best burgers and martinis in New York City. The second floor, where once upon a time the family who owned the tavern lived, has now been turned into a dining room. There are heavy wooden beams, brick walls, and wide-planked wooden floors. Along one side of the wall is a long, old-fashioned bar with lots of brass and colorful bottles of gin and whisky. It's a knockout room, where you can feel New York history the minute you step in the door. It's where Peter and I got married a year and a half after we met.

Peter is Jewish and I'm not, so we were married by a New York federal judge, a friend of my father's. In his e-mail happily and generously agreeing to marry us, our judge said, "Robes or no robes? God or no God?" We decided on robes and no God. To include our religions in the ceremony, we asked Peter's uncle Steven to say a blessing over a challah and for Bess to say a prayer. The rest was civil.

It was October. We put white pumpkins going up the stairs and filled the room with dahlias that were all the colors of an autumn afternoon. The rest was a haze of candles, restaurant white tablecloths, a ton of friends, our family, martinis, and hamburgers.

Ben, who told me to marry someone like me, stepped on my long, flowy dress while giving me a big hug and ripped the hem; Vanessa and Sasha from the Woodstock trip scurried around finding safety pins. I saw my shredded hem tacked together by the good efforts of my beloved friends as good luck. Like rain on a wedding day. Wallace, Antonia, and James had decorated the cake with their own ideas. Wallace chose fireworks; Antonia, fennecs (a fox-like creature); and James, blue sharks with big teeth. They all drank seltzer out of pint glasses and stared in wonder at their three-tiered creation.

I had set up a little altar, decorated with magnolia leaves, using the outline of the old fireplace in the corner of the room. The wall is exposed brick, so the back of the fireplace still sticks out a bit like a mantel. We didn't have a wedding planner. We were playing the evening by ear. When it felt like people had had a drink and settled in a bit, I said to my father, "I think we should get married now." And I started to make my way toward the corner of the room.

"Ish, where are you thinking this will be done? Over there?" he said, pointing to my altar.

"Yeah, it's the old fireplace of the family who lived here," I said, thinking the hearth would be the natural place to do it.

"Ish, two hundred people can't jam in over there, you have to get married in the center of the room. Right here. In front of the bar."

"Dad! In front of the bar?" But I looked around and he was right. Dad had been the advance man for Nelson A. Rockefeller's 1964 presidential campaign, and he knew about rooms and people.

At around 7:00 on October 13, Peter and I were married in the center of the room. Wallace and Antonia milled about our legs while my father held on to James, who was three and who felt uneasy about all the hoopla. Our old and good friends Oscar and Gill stood by our sides, parents and siblings gathered around, and the bartenders tried to disappear behind the piles of crushed ice and shrimp that stood on the bar.

I loved saying the vows again.

chapter 31

As Peter and I grew into our marriage and formed a family, the drive I had to find out what I did wrong my first time around faded. Another relationship was working beautifully. Maybe the divorce really was the first man's fault? Maybe Josiah and I had simply not been meant to be together. What an utter joy to revel in and start a new life with someone I was happily in love with and to sweep all accountability for that other marriage under the heavy, old Persian rug. I could cook meal after meal, play with the kids, make a home, have great sex, work, be a class parent, take up yoga, work, watch movies, and forget about that whole divorce thing and why on earth it happened. Who cared, after all? The past was the past. Blech. But the breakup of a marriage sheds a light on a rather large lump of issues, which you can hide under the rug for only so long. I couldn't escape the fact that I hadn't yet figured out my part in the breakup with Josiah. I knew that I could lose my temper and yell. I knew that I could be too controlling, too worried, too frightened, too jealous, too terrified of losing the connection with someone.

All those extremes are my imperfections. They just are. They helped ruin my first marriage. And did I think just because I was in love with such a wonderful new husband that they would go away? And did I imagine that even if by miracle they didn't appear while I was with the new man in my life that they would never reappear when I was with my kids?

Oh, I hate to write this part, because I wish I were perfect and didn't have to battle with my ugly traits, but slowly, as the years went by after Peter and I were married, my imperfections started to roll in again like a hazardous fog. I was yelling at the children; I felt anxious, overwhelmed, and out of control; frightened that I was going to lose everyone because I wouldn't be wonderful enough to have everyone stay. Why didn't I just feel good and connected like so many friends I saw around me? I felt like other people's insides were made of clay and mine were made of butterflies. What was the matter with me? Why, at the very bottom of my heart, did I sometimes feel so troubled?

As murky as those questions are, here is a list of what I sincerely believe (after many years of looking at myself, especially post-divorce) was affecting my ability to have a successful relationship.

- *Susceptibility to the elements*—hunger, fatigue, being cold. This may sound trite, because it's not psychological, but if I don't eat I am so difficult it could easily ruin a marriage. I get that from my father. He doesn't turn nasty as much as he wilts. All six foot three inches of him starts to slump, and he rubs his face in his hands like it is all about to be over. If that is happening, he is pretty much useless, until you feed him.

Also, lately (and this may be a perimenopause thing), if I don't get a good night's sleep, I'm an ogre, a bad ogre. This truth is a little too hothouse-flower for my taste, but it's a truth, nevertheless. Lack of sleep was screwing up my life.

* *Dyslexia.* From kindergarten through tenth grade, it was hard feeling like I was never as smart as everyone else (which you *are*, you just have technical difficulties). Something kicked in for me when I was sixteen and I got in touch with the I-am-good-at-something side, but until then I wished with all my might that I was not so fucking stupid, which led to insecurity.

* *Insecurity.* I'm insecure.

* *Mothers.* Naomi Judd once said you can't be mad at your mother after the age of thirty-five. I am now forty. And Naomi Judd is correct. You can't stay mad or confused or irritated, it's more fun to just know and love her. However, you can, without anger or judgment, look to the mother for information about why you might do what you do. My mother and I and all of the women in my maternal lineage, going back as far as living memory goes, have had complicated, maybe just WASPy, maybe just kooky experiences with mothering. We try hard to get it right, but generation after generation, something goes wrong. Even though it's the last thing we want to do (and I understand that I am talking about dead people who can't defend

themselves and about my own generous, beloved
mother, as well as myself), we can try as hard as we
might and still somehow make our kids feel unlovable. We shut out or yell or drive too hard. There's
something going on there that isn't great.

• *Drama Queen.* I'm one. And the way I handled feeling
unlovable to my mother or anyone else was to employ
the powerful tool of drama. Did it for years. Crying,
making something about me that really had very
little to do with me, a tantrum here and there followed by depression and anxiety, and some wild
histrionics. Not all the time, but sometimes, and
sometimes big.

Well, I was Goddamned if I was going to yell at my beloved children or alienate my husband or feel miserable
about myself if I didn't have to. But I just couldn't figure it
out by myself. So I got help.

It was humiliating walking into Dr. Tell-it-to-you-straight-
shrink's office five years after my first marriage had ended to
say that I thought I was failing. This shrink is like Judd Hirsch
in the movie *Ordinary People* or like Louis Gossett Jr. in *An Of-
ficer and a Gentleman*, a character who is going to help you, but
not in a lovely, hand-holding way, more in an I'm-going-to-
kick-your-ass-to-kingdom-come-until-you-get-ahold-of-
yourself-and-stop-this-bullshit way. Plus, to help you picture
this: He is my age, Argentinean, and bald.

I told him everything. Every ugly detail. I told him that I
sometimes yelled at the kids without much control. I told him

I got irrationally jealous to the point where I couldn't make myself feel better. I was anxious and was losing tons and tons of sleep. What a waste not to be able to sleep and to yell too loudly in an otherwise happy, albeit complicated, life.

Once the doctor made the connection that I thrived on drama and that I was an actress, he asked me if I could stop the hysterics when I worked.

"Well, yes. But I will say I'm really good at life-ending tears. I've kind of made a career out of it."

"But when the director says 'Stop!', can you?" he asked in his Latin accent.

"Sure. In seconds."

"What do you think of?"

"Well, chocolate ice cream," I said. It's a technique I have been using since acting school. Once I had to cry for four days in a car because my TV character had been in a crash and the trauma of it put her into labor. The lovely, hugely talented and funny actress Mariska Hargitay had to deliver my baby in the ambulance. The two of us bawled for days on end in rubber shattered-glass and fake blood, but when the action was cut and we had to go to lunch, I thought of a chocolate ice cream cone at Billy's in Maine, and it was all over.

"Okay, then. You know when you are going too far, yes? When you are losing control of yourself? Right?"

"Oh, totally." I was terrified that this guy saw the picture so clearly.

"Okay. I want you to think of chocolate ice cream."

I looked at him like You-have-got-to-be-kidding-me.

"You will be able to stop, and that is what you have to do.

Unless someone is bleeding, there's nothing that can't be left alone for ten minutes. Think of chocolate ice cream and stop what you are doing. And in ten minutes, you will be able to handle the circumstances better."

He is correct. I am impulsive, but if I simply pause for a few minutes, I usually get the whole thing much closer to right.

I said I wanted a new road, and he miraculously said that if I worked on it, I could have one. The Drama Mama had been effective in some ways for many years, but now it was time to evolve. And he said that the fact that I was sitting there, admitting there was something I wanted to change, was the best evidence that I could do it.

"I want you to get a ring. When you feel yourself about to take off into this cosmic aloneness, as you say, or when you start to lose your temper, you touch this ring and it will remind you of your new road."

"Well, you don't have to tell me twice to get a ring," I joked, exhausted.

This doctor also told me to make a point of getting seven to eight hours of sleep. No messing around with that.

Prescriptions for changing your life are a gift, but one you have to participate in every day, like a membership to the gym. To actually change, you must work and be ready for your life to be better.

I left the ninety-minute session stunned, and that night I cried hard. I knew I could do it, it wasn't that; it was that finally I had gotten the information I was looking for. I could see my shadow side with a clarity that felt tranquil rather than troubled. The blinders were off, I might even say the chains were off, and I felt raw. Peter held on to me as I cried, explaining to him what I had been doing wrong all these years and what was ahead.

"You know," he said, smoothing the hair back over my ear, "you are not as bad as you think. You are a terrific mom and the best wife I can ever imagine."

"Thanks, babe." I took his hand, which is the same size as mine, and tucked it into my chest. His praise felt like a red flannel blanket being tucked around me, and I lodged myself closer into the crook of his arm. I didn't relax, though; no, I was braced. And, as if it were an unwanted but undeniable premonition, I could feel future pitfalls and missteps and mistakes waiting for me to make. How could I beat my history completely? How could I be strong enough to be a really good wife and mother? *All I want to be is a good wife and mother,* I thought. But parts of the job didn't come easily to me. Yet before despair could leak in through that secure flannel blanket, I thought of one good thing about myself: *I try.* And I would try my best every day. That notion felt like something I could trust, and because of it I knew I wouldn't lose Peter and I wouldn't hurt my kids, and that was happiness.

When I picture what's ahead now, this new road that I wanted so much, it's wide and made of dirt. There are embedded rocks in it and wild weeds growing on the sides that sometimes creep in toward the middle. There are tall, older trees that provide a place to sit and lean on now and again, but mostly the way is clear. I can see far, far down the road, and I know who is on the road with me. And the sun is shining.

epilogue

I am forever amazed at how, no matter if they are positive or negative, all the people in your life and everything that happens to you eventually make sense. Many things are not perfect, but they are good enough, and good enough is all you really need to be. (Read Andre Agassi's memoir. You cannot imagine how many matches that guy lost, yet he was still a champion.)

Of course, it's tough to teach this long view to children.

One evening, Wallace was at his desk slogging through writing everything there is to know about the days in the week and the months in the year. S-E-P-T-E-M-B-E-R. I hovered and squirmed as I watched his letters get bigger and veer every which way across the page. I tried to help him, got in his way, infuriated him, wouldn't let him be. Just terrible parenting, but I couldn't help it; at that point I wasn't prac-ticed at thinking about chocolate ice cream and stepping away for five minutes. Wallace became more and more miserable, and I felt all of his anxiety and worry and anger about stupid homework-that-you-can't-do-for-him. Soon, we were both beside ourselves.

I am dyslexic and so is this son. I'd hoped and prayed that my kids would both get the straight-A gene from their father, but as it happened, the older one got my find-it-almost-impossible-to-read-and-write gene. He was now in second grade and there was a lot of homework. He goes to a marvelous public school that is a vibrant, happy, huge, and overcrowded but abundantly friendly place. It is one block from where we live and it is mostly exactly what he needs. The school's motto is "One Family Under the Sun," and if my children learn that lesson, I will feel the school has done its job.

A big bummer about having learning disabilities like the ones that my son and I share is that you experience massive frustration. You are smart, sensitive, feel a million ways about subjects, see the big picture, have interests and opinions, but you can't read about what interests you or express yourself about what interests you. It sucks.

"I HATE THIS STUPID, IDIOT WRITING! I CAN'T DO IT! I HATE ENGLISH AND LETTERS AND IT'S AN IDIOT!" Wallace howled. ("Idiot" is a very bad word in our house; to Wallace, it was as if he were yelling "stupid-mother-bitch-cunt-fucker.")

"My sweetheart, I know. I *know* how hard it is, but you just have to do it," I said, desperately grasping for anything to say and knowing that I wasn't handling it right. Mikey, our male, twenty-three-year-old babysitter, walked by and looked at me like I was barking up the wrong tree, which I was. And because I was offering my son nothing, he became even more frus-

trated and just screamed: "AHHHHHHHHHHHHHHHH-
HHHHHHHHHHHHHHHH."

"Wallace!" I barked, "Marge"—our neighbor—"is going
to call the cops and we all will get arrested if you yell like
that!"

Nice. The kid is in misery and feeling alone in the world,
and I say the cops are going to take him and me away. Smooth
move, Isabel.

Wallace looked at me with all the pain in the world in his
big, root-beer-brown eyes. Help me, he was saying—but I
couldn't. I felt sick and mad at myself for having dyslexia and
giving it to him. I felt lost and like I was about to run away or
yell at him because I couldn't help him. Where in the world
was someone who could help him? Almost in tears myself,
feeling like a failure, inexplicably, I thought of Skype. I thought
of my boy's English professor father and the miracle advance-
ment in technology, Skype! I am convinced that Skype is going to save families of divorce. I ran into the other room and
called Josiah in Ohio. He was in his office, as usual.

"Wallace is freaking out about homework and I can't help
him."

"WHaaaaaaa Yiiiiiieaaahhhhhh. IDIOT! IDIOT!!!"

"Yeah, I can hear him," Josiah said. "Let's Skype."

Relieved, I opened the computer, heard the *Jetsons* noises
of Josiah dialing me up across the Internet, and just as if I'd
taken that first sip of coffee, or drag of a cigarette (I quit fifteen years ago, but I will never forget what a relief that first
drag was), my body relaxed when I saw the boys' father through
the screen in his office in Ohio.

"Wallace! Daddy is on Skype! Come in here!"

My distressed boy came rushing in. I couldn't help him, he couldn't help himself, but there was his dad.

"Hey, sweetheart. Having a hard time, huh?"

"Yes! I can't do it, Dad! It's too much. I've been writing all day and I can't do it." He sobbed in his chair.

They worked it out. Apparently, Josiah gets overwhelmed, too. He has kitchen timers all over his office so he can manage the time. He regulates the amounts of time he has to do something he feels is too hard, and he uses a cool little kitchen gadget to do it. He had about four in his office. He showed all of them to Wallace.

"Where can I get one?" Wallace said, looking intently and eagerly at the one his father was showing him from every angle all the way from Ohio.

"Oh goodness, I have one! I have one!" I said, remembering an impulse buy I'd made at Zabar's, a cooking store, and I ran into the kitchen to get it—my small contribution—and gave it to my boy. I stood about six feet away from this process, with my hands clutched and knees slightly bent, like I was watching a kids' soccer game.

"Dad, I'll set mine and you set yours!"

"Okay, good idea. I have something to finish up here. Wanna do our work together?"

"Yeah, yeah. Let's set it for four minutes and thirty-seven seconds!"

"Okay, my boy. Good idea."

They set their timers with the same expression of concentration on each of their faces and got to work, heads down, quietly and contentedly, with the computer between them.

It is hard raising kiddos together without being married. Life's daily coordinates are constantly changing; but you can't give up or you will lose all the value that is more than likely there in doing the job together as you once set out to do. And it's really great, if you can, to be friends.

* * *

And here's a last story, a sad one, but with happiness laced in it. It's a part of a full, real life. My real life with Peter.

Right after Peter and I married, I got pregnant. Just like that. It took us by surprise. One night I was watching a Woody Allen movie, *Match Point*, and right in the middle of it I had the distinct feeling I was pregnant. Without saying anything, I got up, went to our bathroom, and took a pregnancy test.

"Hey, babe," I said, leaning back into the doorway of the room where he was working, "I'm pregnant."

It was sort of a miracle that we made a baby at all, as my body is closing up shop in that department and Peter had issues, too. But we had truly conceived, with abandon and in love.

Almost a year before that I had been doing a movie in New Orleans and Peter was in New York. We were on the phone, watching the U.S. Open together on TV. At the Open, they were paying a big tribute to Billie Jean King.

"What an amazing woman," we both kept exclaiming.

"If we ever have a baby, let's name him or her Billie," Peter said. That's one of the thousand things Peter has said that made me fall and fall and fall in love with him.

"It's a plan, babe," I said, giddy.

So a year later, we had a little Billie growing. That baby

grew for three months, then at the twelve-week sonogram, I saw clearly that there was no heartbeat. The world fell away. Once again I'd lost the context of my life. Peter rushed to me from his office. I had never before held on to anyone like that or felt as joined to anyone.

The day after the D&C, I bought all of our Christmas presents in the pouring rain in Times Square.

The following day, the bleeding started while the boys were in school. Alone, I curled up in the corner of the sofa where the children watch TV, with my sons' pajamas wrapped around my arms like snakes. I was inconsolable. Like many women who have tried to describe this before, I really can't.

We were having a baby together, then we weren't.

We lost a whole life, and it was so big, and not a day goes by when I don't think about what could have been—but what we realized together was that we had conceived a baby out of good love. And good love holds everything: It holds the miracle of making a baby and the tragedy of losing it. It holds marriage, kids, divorce, parents, doing dishes, school graduations, taxes, weeding a garden, recommending articles, As, Bs, Cs, Ds, and Fs, sex, broken arms, getting with the program, rock and roll, public transportation, new jobs, fortieth birthdays, first birthdays, family visits, ordering badly, walking, leaking roofs, the tide, sick parents, bath oil, dark storms, bringing home pals, back pain, the *New York Times*, crying hard, planting bulbs, reading maps, taking naps, allowance, Yosemite, leftover turkey sandwiches, writing "5"s, touching base, tennis, teenage hearts, repainting hallways, dogs, best friends, sides of the bed, starry nights—and dark ones, too.

It says in the Bible that love endures, and when I think about my boys and their father and their love, I have to believe that love surely does endure, surviving metamorphoses and steep climbs.

But good love—good love holds it all, and finally, it held me.

acknowledgments

I am very aware of all the help I have received getting this book into the world. It took brains, ideas, energy, time, creativity, and devotion from many people other than me, and for all of that, I am forever filled with gratitude.

I would right away like to thank, from the bottom of my heart, Bill Clegg for his inspiring, wonderfully positive, and generous involvement in my life. I owe so many past and future chapters to you. You changed everything, and I just love, admire, and thank you tremendously.

I would like to enthusiastically thank Barbara Jones. Thank you for all of your very hard work and wise words. I admire you greatly not only as an editor but as a woman and mother.

Thank you, Ellen Archer, for your generous support and for "A Love Story."

I give many thanks to Claire McKean for your careful production management of my book, and Laura Klynstra for this cheerful cover. Also, Kate Griffin, Betsy Wilson, and Shaun Dolan for your fine help all year. Thank you, Allison McGeehon and Caroline Riordan, for looking forward to this book before it was even born, then promoting it so enthusiastically.

Thank you to my treasured friends, many of whom are in this book, many of whom are not. I love you all so very much.

Thank you wholeheartedly to Sharon Kozberg, Milton Wainberg, Judith Aguda, Ken Treusch, *Law & Order SVU*, PS 87, and 275.

A big fat thank-you to the invaluable and marvelous Eugene Michael Santiago.

Thank you to L, D, and P for your patience and understanding. Last one, promise.

As for the families: Gillies, Lattman, Rogers, and Harrison, thank you for your consistent love and support. I am very lucky and happy to be a part of the herds.

Mum and Dad, you are marvelous parents. A lifetime of thank-yous and loves to you.

To Peter: There is not a day that goes by when my breath doesn't get taken away by how much I love the talented, hardworking, kind, funny, dead-sexy you. Thank you, my love, for all of it.

And finally, to the wonderful, smart, beautiful, patient children that I am so proud to be the mother (and stepmother) of: Thank you, my darlings. You all shine.